TUCCI

TASTE

Before Stanley Tucci became a household name with *The Devil Wears Prada*, *The Hunger Games*, and the perfect Negroni, he grew up in an Italian American family that spent every night around the table. He shared the magic of those meals in *The Tucci Cookbook* and *The Tucci Table*, and now he takes us beyond the recipes and into the stories behind them.

Taste is a reflection on the intersection of food and life, filled with anecdotes about growing up in Westchester, New York, preparing for and filming the foodie films *Big Night* and *Julie and Julia*, falling in love over dinner, and teaming up with his wife to create conversation-starting meals for their children. Each morsel of this gastronomic journey through good times and bad, five-star meals and burnt dishes, is as heartfelt and delicious as the last.

Written with Stanley's signature wry humour, *Taste* is a heartwarming read that will be irresistible for anyone who knows the power of a home-cooked meal.

About the author

Stanley Tucci is an actor, writer, director and producer. He has directed five films and appeared in over seventy films, countless television shows, and a dozen plays on and off Broadway. He has been nominated for an Academy Award, a Tony, and a spoken-word Grammy; is a winner of two Golden Globes and two Emmys; and has received numerous other critical and professional awards and accolades.

By the same author

The Tucci Cookbook
The Tucci Table

TASTE

My Life
Through Food

STANLEY TUCCI

FIG TREE
an imprint of
PENGUIN BOOKS

FIG TREE

UK | USA | Canada | Ireland | Australia
India | New Zealand | South Africa

Fig Tree is part of the Penguin Random House group of companies
whose addresses can be found at global.penguinrandomhouse.com.

First published in the United States of America by Gallery Books 2021
First published in Great Britain by Fig Tree 2021

005

Copyright © Stanley Tucci, 2021

The moral right of the author has been asserted

Set in 11/18 pt Adobe Garamond Pro
Typeset by Jouve (UK), Milton Keynes
Printed and bound in Great Britain by Clays Ltd, Elcograf S.p.A.

The authorized representative in the EEA is Penguin Random House Ireland,
Morrison Chambers, 32 Nassau Street, Dublin D02 YH68

A CIP catalogue record for this book is available from the British Library

ISBN: 978–0–241–50099–6

www.greenpenguin.co.uk

To my incredible parents, for giving me and my sisters so much,
and for teaching me how and why to love life and food.

To my wife, Felicity, for her extraordinary mind,
her open heart, and her appetite.

And to my gorgeous children, may they always find happiness
wherever they are, especially at the table.

TASTE

An Introduction

I grew up in an Italian family that, not unusually, put great import on food. My mother's cooking was extraordinary and there was a daily, almost obsessive focus on the quality of the ingredients, their careful preparation, the passing on of family recipes, and cultural culinary traditions. About twenty-five years ago I made a film called *Big Night* that told the story of two Italian brothers struggling to keep their restaurant going. It ended up heightening my interest in all things culinary and catapulted me into places, relationships and experiences I never thought I would have. To this day, restaurateurs, chefs and food lovers all around the world tell me how much they like and are inspired by the film. I am more than flattered and almost embarrassed by their kind words, and, in the case of many, their generosity. I am always thrilled and thankful for such moments, as I so admire anyone who runs a good restaurant, decides to lead the gruelling life of a chef, or simply takes the time and effort to make a good meal for people they love.

My love of food and all that it encompasses only continues to grow every year. It has led me to write cookbooks, become involved in food-related charities, make a documentary series, and it is ultimately what brought my wife Felicity and me together.

As it is fair to say that I now probably spend more time thinking about and focusing on food than I do on acting, as is evidenced by some of my recent performances, it seems appropriate that this primary passion take yet another form: that of a memoir of sorts. The following pages offer a taste of such a memoir. I hope you find them palatable. (More puns to follow.)

S. Tucci
London, 2021

Westchester County, New York, mid-1960s

*M*y mother and I are sitting on the floor in our small living room. I am around six years old. I am playing with a set of blocks and my mother is ironing. The TV is tuned to a cooking show.

ME: What is she doing?

MY MOTHER: She's cooking.

ME: What?

MY MOTHER: She's cooking.

ME: I know. I mean . . . *what* is she cooking?

MY MOTHER: Oh, she's cooking a duck.

ME: A *duck?!!*

MY MOTHER: Yep.

ME: From a pond?

MY MOTHER: I guess so. I don't know.

I am silent. I build; she irons.

MY MOTHER: How are you feeling?

ME: I think, better.

She feels my forehead.

MY MOTHER: Well, I think your fever's gone down.

ME: Will I have to go to school tomorrow?

MY MOTHER: We'll see.

A silence as we watch the TV.

MY MOTHER: Are you hungry?

I nod.

MY MOTHER: What would you like?

ME: I don't know.

MY MOTHER: A sandwich?

I offer no response.

MY MOTHER: Would you like a sandwich?

ME: Ummm . . .

MY MOTHER: How about a peanut butter and jelly sandwich.

ME: Ummmm . . . yeah.

My mother raises her eyebrows. I notice.

ME: Yes, please.

MY MOTHER: Okay. When the show is over in ten minutes I will make you a sandwich.

ME: But I'm hungry now.

My mother just looks at me, eyebrows raised even higher. I go back to my blocks.

MY MOTHER: Do you remember that show when she made crêpes?

ME: What?

MY MOTHER: Crêpes. Those pancakes.

ME: Ummmm . . .

MY MOTHER: That I make sometimes . . .

ME: I don't know.

MY MOTHER: Well, anyway, do you want to help me make them this weekend?

ME: Ummm, sure.

A beat.

ME: Why is she cooking a duck?

MY MOTHER: I guess she *likes* duck.

A silence. We watch the TV.

ME: Do *you* like duck?

MY MOTHER: I've never really had it.

A beat.

ME: Do *I* like duck?

MY MOTHER: I don't know. *Do* you?

ME: Have I had it?

MY MOTHER: No.

ME: Then I probably don't like it.

MY MOTHER: You can't know if you don't like something if you haven't had it. You have to try it. You have to try everything.

ME: Mmm. Maybe later. Some day, when I'm older, maybe.

I watch the TV. My mother looks at me and can't help but smile. A silence. The show ends and we go to the kitchen.

She makes a peanut butter and jelly sandwich for me, which I eat ravenously. She watches.

MY MOTHER: Wow, you *were* hungry.

I nod with a mouth full of food and then speak, mouth still full.

ME: What are we having for dinner?

MY MOTHER: Pork chops.

ME: Awwwww!!! No. I don't *like* pork chops.

My mother sighs.

MY MOTHER: Well, why don't you go next door and see what the neighbours are having?

I sigh dramatically and continue eating the sandwich. My mother smiles and begins to clean the kitchen.

'What Can I Get You to Drink?'

This question was asked by my father immediately upon any guest's arrival in our home. He loved – and still, at age ninety-one, does love – a good cocktail. He's never gone in for anything fancy, but our home always had a very well-stocked bar that contained the necessary liquors for any drink a guest requested. My father himself usually just drank Scotch on the rocks in the autumn and winter, gin and tonics or beer in the summer, and of course wine with every meal no matter what the season. I loved to watch him make a drink for our guests, and when I came of age, this task was passed on to me and I proudly accepted it.

Today, I also ask the same question when guests cross my threshold and take great joy in mixing up whatever tipple floats their boat. I also make one for myself every evening. What form it might take differs with the seasons and my temperament. Sometimes it's a Martini, other times a vodka tonic, on occasion a cold sake, a whiskey sour, or a simple Scotch on the rocks, and so on and so on. This past year I began a relationship with a Negroni and I am happy to say it's going very well.

Here's how I make one.

A Negroni – Up

– SERVES 1 –

50ml gin

25ml Campari

25ml good sweet vermouth

Ice

1 orange slice

- Pour all the booze into a cocktail shaker filled with ice.

- Shake it well.

- Strain it into a coupe.

- Garnish with a slice of orange.

- Sit down.

- Drink it.

- The sun is now in your stomach.

(There are those who consider serving this cocktail 'straight up' to be an act of spirituous heresy. But they needn't get so upset. I never planned on inviting them to my home anyway.)

1

I grew up in Katonah, New York, a beautiful town about sixty miles north of Manhattan. We moved there when I was three years of age from Peekskill, New York, a small city with a large Italian population on the Hudson River where my father's family had settled after emigrating from Calabria. My mother's family, also from Calabria, lived in neighbouring Verplanck, a town composed of mostly Italian and Irish immigrants. My parents, Joan Tropiano and Stanley Tucci the Second, met at a picnic in 1959, and my father proposed a few months later. They married soon afterwards and I was born ten months after their wedding day. Clearly they were in a hurry to breed. My sister Gina followed three years later, and my sister Christine three years after that. We lived in a three-bedroom contemporary house at the top of a hill on a cul-de-sac mostly surrounded by woods. My father was the head of the art department at a high school a few towns away, and my mother worked in the office there. My sisters and I went to our local elementary, junior high and high schools.

In the sixties and seventies, the suburbs of northern Westchester were not nearly as densely populated as they are today and were a rather ideal place to grow up. My sisters and I had a great group of friends who lived on our road and close by with whom we played daily and almost exclusively out of doors. There were no video games or mobile phones, and television was only watched on occasion. Instead we played in each other's yards or the nearby fields, but mostly in the surrounding woods, throughout the year. The woods had everything to offer us. Endless trees to climb and in which 'forts' could be built, swamps to trudge through or skate on when frozen, Revolutionary War era stone walls to climb, and hills to sled down when they were covered in the deep snow that used to fall consistently every winter.

Now that I am in the autumn of my years (I have just turned sixty, so that might be edging towards mid- to late autumn), I often wish I could return to those times, that place, and my innocent, curious, energetic self. I would also like to go back if only to retrieve my beautiful head of hair.

The carefree activities out of doors in all kinds of weather were a wonderful part of my childhood, but what was even *more* wonderful was what and how my family cooked and ate.

―――――――

Food, its preparation, serving and ingesting, was the primary activity and the main topic of conversation in my household growing up. My mother insists that she was capable of little more than boiling water when she married my father. If this is true, she has more than made up for this shortcoming over the last half century. I can honestly say that on the four-burner electric stove she used through my childhood and on the gas hob that replaced it many years later, she has never cooked a bad meal. Not once. The focus of her cooking is Italian, primarily recipes from her family or my father's family. (However, she was never afraid to branch out into the cuisine of northern Italy. Her risotto Milanese is still one of the best I have ever tasted.)

Over the years she also perfected a few dishes from other countries, which became staples of her repertoire. One year paella appeared, cooked and served in an elegant orange and white Dansk casserole dish. Brimming with clams, mussels, shrimp, chicken and lobster tails (at the time lobster was somewhat affordable), it became a special treat for years to come. Crêpes made their way on to our table at some point in the early 1970s, no doubt inspired by Julia Child. Light and airy, they were stuffed with chicken in a béchamel sauce and greedily devoured by us all. Rich, thick chili con carne appeared every now and again, speckled with green and red peppers, its meat made unctuous by rich red tomatoes and olive oil. This dish was often specifically made for some neighbour's annual Super Bowl party. We never threw any such fête, as no one in the house was in any way a football fan.

It should be obvious by now that when I was young, my mother spent most of her waking time in the kitchen, and she still does to this day. Cooking for her is at once a creative outlet and a way of feeding her family well. Her cooking, like that of any great cook or chef, is proof that culinary creativity may be the most perfect art form. It allows for free personal expression like painting, musical composition or writing and yet fulfils a most practical need: the need to eat. Edible art. What could be better?

Because of my mother's culinary prowess, eating at neighbours' houses as a kid was always a bit of a struggle. The meals were bland or just plain not good. However, my friends were more than happy to spend time at *our* table. They knew the food at our house was something quite special. The ingredients had been carefully chosen or grown according to the season; each dish had a cultural history and was lovingly made.

It was not only the food itself in which they delighted but the passion with which it was made and presented, as well as the joy our family took in its consumption. The moans of satisfaction that the meal elicited from us were enough to convince one to enjoy the meal even if one wasn't already. Between moans there was the usual discussion of how and why it was all so delicious. 'The best you've ever made, Joan,' my father would say about one dish or another every night. We, my two sisters and I, would agree as my mother would mutter something about there not being enough salt or something needing more cooking time, or saying, 'It's a little dry, don't you think?' and so on.

This discourse was followed by stories of previous meals, imagined ones, or desired preferences for those to come, and before one knew it the meal had ended and little else had been discussed other than food. Politics, luckily, were quite low on the list. No matter what one ate, even if it was just cold cuts and olives from a delicatessen, it was elevated to a new level of flavour in my parents' home. A college friend once said to me when eating prosciutto, bread and cheese in my first apartment in New York City, 'Stan, how come even though I buy the same stuff from the same store, it tastes better when I'm at your house?'

'You should visit my parents,' was my reply.

In Italian families, nothing is discussed, ruminated on or joked about as much as food (except death, but I'll save that subject for another book), and hence there are quite a few food-related expressions that have been passed down through my family over many generations that I continue to use to this day myself.

My father is a voracious eater, and during dinner, while savouring his food (in truth he would be eating it very quickly, as savouring is something neither he nor I practises, although I suppose we are experts in the postprandial savour), he would inevitably utter the rhetorical question, 'My God, what does the rest of the world eat?!!!'

To me, given the quality of the food, it was a more than fair question. When he was told that dinner was soon to be served, he would take a sip of his Scotch, slam the glass on the butcher-block counter, and loudly pronounce, '*Buono! Perche io ho une fame che parla con Dio!*'

This translates as . . .

'*Good! Because I have a hunger that speaks with God!*'

God has paid little attention, it seems, to truly sating him, as my father's biblically proportioned hunger returns every evening.

When he was young, my father would, as all children do, ask the question, 'Mom, what's for dinner?'

His very sweet mother (sweet by all accounts, for I didn't know her well as I was only seven when she died) would respond with, '*Cazzi e patate.*'

This translates directly as '*Dicks and potatoes.*' In other words, 'Leave me alone,' or 'Bugger off,' as the Brits might say. In today's 'PC' climate, a social worker might be brought into a household to oversee parents who spoke to their children this way. One could only hope for a social worker with Italian roots.

When we were young, whenever my sisters or I complained about a certain meal my mother had lovingly made, she would suggest rather tersely that we go see what the neighbours were cooking. And that, as they say, put an end to that. The reason being, as I said, having eaten at many of our neighbours' homes, we had no desire to revisit their tables. In our home each day of the week a delicious and well-balanced meal appeared from the kitchen, and no matter how much we might gripe about our personal aversions to broccoli, fish, salad or pork chops, we knew how lucky we were. Yet, for all of her posturing about insisting we go skulking about the neighbourhood to sniff out a better meal when we complained about hers, my mother was very well aware of our individual likes and dislikes and she did her best to make, if not a main dish, then a couple of side dishes every night that satisfied everyone. A typical meal might consist of a bowl of pasta with broccoli, breaded veal cutlets with sautéd *zucchine* on the side, and a green salad. Within that array of dishes there was something for all of us. My sister

Christine loved meat, Gina preferred pasta and vegetables, and I ate basically everything that wasn't nailed down. The next night's fare might be chicken *alla cacciatore*, with a side of rice, sautéd escarole and cabbage salad, and so on and so on. How my mother turned out these amazing, diverse, healthy meals night after night while having a full-time job is beyond me.

By the time Friday rolled around, the household budget had been stretched to its limit, relegating end-of-the-week meals to simple, inexpensive fare. However, given the innate Italian facility to create something substantial out of practically nothing, we hardly suffered. Fridays were often also the only night that my father would cook, in order to give my mother a much-needed rest. She in turn became the sous-chef, facilitating as necessary. A usual Friday night dinner would be one of a handful of dishes that my father was most comfortable preparing. The simplest and most often prepared was *pasta con aglio e olio* (pasta with garlic and olive oil).

Here it is.

Pasta con Aglio e Olio

– SERVES 4 –

3 garlic cloves, cut into thirds
4 tablespoons olive oil
500g spaghetti

- Sauté the garlic in the olive oil until lightly browned.

- Boil the spaghetti until it's al dente.

- Drain the spaghetti and toss with the oil and garlic mixture.

- Add salt, pepper and paprika to taste.

- Cheese is not allowed.

My father's second go-to Friday night dish was *uova fra diavolo*. For egg-obsessed people, like my father and me, nothing could be as desirous as this rich, visually stunning meal. Imagine a deep frying pan of delicate red-orange marinara sauce (made with more onions than usual for extra sweetness), in which six to eight eggs are poached. The result, as its name implies, is positively sinful. This was accompanied by lightly toasted Italian bread and followed by a green salad. Here is the recipe.

Eggs with Tomato

– SERVES 2 –

50ml olive oil
1 medium to large onion, thinly sliced
200g canned whole plum tomatoes
4 large eggs
Sea salt and freshly ground black pepper

- Warm the olive oil in a medium non-stick frying pan over a medium heat. Add the onion and cook until soft, about 3 minutes. Add the tomatoes, crushing them with your hand or the back of a slotted spoon. Cook, stirring occasionally, until the tomatoes have sweetened, about 20 minutes.

- Gently break the eggs into the pan and cover. Decrease the heat to medium-low and cook until the whites are opaque and the yolks are moderately firm, about 5 minutes. Serve immediately, seasoned with salt and pepper to taste.

The third Friday favourite was fried meatballs. This was a meal my parents would make together, my mother preparing the meatball mixture, rolling them, and my father frying them slowly in olive oil. Many meatballs were cooked on a Friday evening, as half were to be eaten that night and the other half were to be used for the Sunday 'ragù'. Those eaten on Friday night were served 'nude', or, in other words, without any sauce at all. They were accompanied by a fresh green salad and Italian bread. It was only when this meal was served that butter made a rare appearance on our table.* When spread on

---

* As butter is not a large part of the southern Italian pantry, it was seldom seen at our table. Bread was never buttered unless it was to be eaten alone as a snack. Bread was used at meals to soak up remaining sauce from a pasta, meat or poultry dish. The thinking is that buttered bread only corrupts the flavours of the leftover sauce.

Italian bread, it was a sweet and soft complement to the crusty meatballs.*

I remember those Friday night meals with great fondness, as there was a more relaxed feeling throughout the house. The work and school week had ended, and a weekend spent with friends and the inevitable Friday or Saturday night sleepover lay ahead for me and my sisters, while my parents looked forward to dinner parties at home or away. We knew that Sunday morning's painfully portentous Catholic mass loomed, but we were well comforted by the thought that the remaining meatballs cooked on Friday evening would be given a new and delicious life in my mother's *ragù* that afternoon.

---

* Regarding the use of bread, some argue that the Florentines make unsalted bread to this day so that it might be as 'neutral'-tasting as possible, in order to maintain the integrity of the sauce it absorbs. Others argue that the lack of salt in Florentine bread is because unsalted bread lasts longer, or it's the result of an innate or inherited Tuscan parsimony stemming from a time when Italy was divided into city-states and wars were fought over necessary and coveted commodities such as salt, which was very dear. When we lived in Florence we never could get used to the unsalted bread, which we found dry and tasteless. I must confess that sometimes I think the best bread in Italy is in France.

2

Like many suburban saplings raised in 1960s America, I would bring lunch to school every day. It was a rare occasion that I would buy a lunch the cafeteria provided. This was for two reasons. One, it was cost-prohibitive for my parents to do so, and two, the food the cafeteria served was dreadful. Anyone growing up at this time anywhere in America knows what I mean, and therefore I need not elaborate. (I will confess, however, to a penchant for the excessively glutinous white rice, served by way of an old-fashioned ice-cream scooper and deposited as a near-perfect sphere in a tiny pastel melamine bowl.)

Now, there were those students who bought lunch either regularly or on occasion. I, however, was only given money (five to ten cents) solely for the purchase of a half pint of milk. (My lactose intolerance was, as yet, undiscovered.)

Though many of my friends brought their lunches, the contents of my lunch box differed significantly from those of my peers. A prime example of my portable childhood lunch, lovingly packed into a pop-image-themed metal container (a.k.a. a Partridge Family or Batman lunch box), would be something akin to the following:

A scrambled egg, fried potato and sautéd sweet green pepper sandwich on two slices of Italian bread or in a 'wedge' or a 'hero', which is a long loaf of Italian bread sliced horizontally and filled with whatever you choose to fill it with. In Philadelphia they are called 'hoagies'.

One piece of fruit. (Apple, pear or orange.)

One highly processed, pre-packaged, store-bought dessert. (Twinkie, Devil Dog, Ring Ding or Ho Ho. The names of which in retrospect seem as inappropriate as their ingredients.)

The fruit and the dessert were standard fare, but it was the sandwiches that were the marvel, and oftentimes made me the envy of my friends.

My dear friend Ricky S——— and I would trade sandwiches every now and again. The reason for this was that he was given a Marshmallow Fluff sandwich on white bread every day of grade school. (Today this would be considered a form of child abuse.) However, in those days no one cared – least of all me, who was more than happy to relinquish my gourmet fare for the unhealthiest schmear between two slices of bread known to man. I am sure he was equally happy to ingest something from which he could derive midday nourishment for once in his very white life. It is important to note that for the most part my exotic and coveted lunches were directly related to the previous night's dinner. A typical week of said lunches might have looked something like this:

Monday: *Meatball wedge. As we had meatballs in a slow-cooked, homemade,* ragù *with pasta for Sunday dinner, this lunch was a natural choice.*

Tuesday: *Chicken cutlets on Italian bread or a wedge with the smallest amount of butter or mayo and lettuce.*

Wednesday: *Eggplant parmigiana wedge. The eggplant parmigiana was not breaded. It was made in light tomato sauce, had very little cheese, and incorporated thinly sliced potatoes.*

Thursday: *Veal cutlet sandwich or wedge with a small amount of butter and lettuce. This was in the days of affordable veal.*

Friday: *Scrambled egg, pepper and potato wedge. As the food budget was wearing thin by the end of the week, this was an inexpensive lunch my mother might whip up on Thursday night after a simple dinner of pasta and salad.*

Lunches on the weekends were catch as catch can. Whether friends were at my house or vice versa, we would raid the fridge and make stacks of peanut butter and jelly sandwiches. As we got older, we would make sandwiches of every ilk: tuna salad, bologna and mustard, ham and cheese, liverwurst and red onion, turkey breast and mayo, American cheese and mayo, all on whatever bread was available (sliced white, Italian, bagels, kaiser rolls, etc.). We ravaged jars of dill pickles and sweet gherkins, bags of Ruffles potato chips and Fritos. We washed it all down with gallons of milk, orange juice, apple juice or lemonade (did any of us ever drink water?). For dessert we emptied the freezers of ice pops of every unnatural colour and flavouring. During school breaks we did the same, but in winter we added hot chocolate (Swiss Miss, with little marshmallows, from individual packets) to our gluttonous midday rampages.

During summer vacations we followed the same routine like crazed ants at an endless picnic. I don't remember anyone in our neighbour-hood ever going on an extended summer vacation, so we all just hung around together for those two humid months, going from one dwelling to another, eating our own and each other's parents out of house and home. I found summer vacations so joyful. The days were long, allow-ing us to play outside until nine p.m., at which point we would have already negotiated a sleepover at one or another of our homes so that we might never be parted even in slumber. Summertime also brought my favourite holiday, besides Christmas: Independence Day, also known as the Fourth of July.

When I was a boy, Fourth of July celebrations were very important in our family. At this time all or most of my family members who had been part of the great wave of Italian immigrants were still alive. Compared to the abject poverty of the Italian south, America held for them everything Italy could not offer or would not allow. It was in America that their dreams of a new and successful life came true.

They created Italian enclaves all over the country by sending for family and friends once work had been secured. America gave them the best of both worlds: a country where prospects were many, and the opportunity to surround themselves with extended family. In this new world, they would birth new generations who had options available to them never thought possible in the poor and corrupt towns of southern Italy. In America they worked together, grew together, and sometimes grew apart together.

Food was the connective tissue that brought them, again and again, into each other's homes, backyards, front porches, campsites, beaches and hearts. The lubricant that is wine ameliorated any squeaky emotional wheels, just as at times it was fuel for any dark and dormant emotional fires.

I remember many of these Independence Day celebrations being held at our house in northern Westchester. We would spend days preparing for the onslaught of relatives from both sides. Out of paper, string and poster board my father would make all of the decorations, from hand-painted pennants to red, white and blue stovepipe hats. With the welding equipment he used to make steel sculpture; he would cut fifty-gallon drums in half lengthwise and place them on sawhorses. They were then filled with charcoal and old steel fridge/freezer shelves were placed across the top, thus creating two enormous barbecues. Over these makeshift grills, the ubiquitous hamburgers and hot dogs were cooked alongside Italian sausages, a simple culinary representation of the melding of two distinctive cultures. The sausages were served on long wedges with slowly sautéed onions and red and green peppers. Jug wine was served, as well as glasses of beer straight from a frigid keg. In those days the ice came in blocks, not in bags of cubes, and as a young boy I relished the task of breaking it into smaller chunks with a deadly ice pick so that they would fit around the portly beer keg that sat in a basin wrapped in thick canvas, waiting to be tapped. For dessert, besides peaches soaked in wine, my mother always served a homemade rectangular sponge cake decorated with the Stars and Stripes. The surface was covered in white icing, with fresh straw-berries comprising the red stripes and blueberries making up the blue field behind the stars.

Music followed dinner as surely as games of horseshoes and bocce preceded it. Uncles on mandolin or piano sang old Italian folk songs or Italian versions of bygone American ditties, like 'Darktown Strutters' Ball'. These, along with a few American classics like 'Yankee Doodle' and 'You're a Grand Old Flag', created the perfect accompaniment to three generations bound by Italian traditions who'd come together to celebrate the quintessential American holiday.

As more and more of the first-generation immigrants passed away, the Fourth of July seemed to become less and less important. We still celebrated it, but certainly not in the numbers or with the same passion we once had. As my generation reached early adult-hood, we began to form our own political opinions, which were usually not in keeping with those of many of the older generations, who were rather conservative and still believed that America was the greatest country in the world no matter what. After the horror of the 9/11 attacks, these political differences were exacerbated. For me and some of the more liberal family members, patriotism seemed to have been monopolized by those with hawkish views of how to right that terrible wrong and who waved the American flag more like a weapon than a symbol of freedom, acceptance and possibility. We were becoming once again a country where immigrants were vilified and disagreeing with the government's wars in the Middle East was practically tantamount to treason. Ultraconservatives even started calling french fries 'Freedom Fries' as well as boycotting and even smashing bottles of French wine because the French refused to send troops to fight alongside the United States in Iraq. I wish they had just sent them to me. Not the troops, the wine. I am hoping now, as I write this, that those days will soon be behind us.

Now that I spend most of my time in London, I must admit celebrating American Independence Day is a tad uncomfortable for one fairly obvious reason: the colonists won and the British lost. (I know the war was a long time ago, but I never quite know how to celebrate that victorious day here without feeling like I'm rubbing it in some Brit's face – like my in-laws.) However, during the Obama administration, my family and I were fortunate enough to be invited to two July Fourth fêtes at Winfield House in Regent's Park, the home of the American ambassador. These were lovely, casually posh daytime affairs for expats (a nice word for immigrants) and their families, complete with American military bands, jazz singers, and all the traditional American foods one could eat.

How ironic that in England, of all places, on these two occasions I would be reminded of all the positive aspects of this important

American day. Taking part in joyous celebrations of American democracy on foreign soil made me long for a time in my youth when the sausage and peppers of Italian immigrants sat peacefully on the grill alongside their American cousins, the hot dog and the hamburger.

———————

My maternal grandmother, Concetta, was one of the funniest and most generous people I've ever met. She was also an extraordinary cook. Her parents emigrated from Calabria when she was three years of age to Verplanck, New York, a small town about forty miles north of Manhattan. She was taught to cook by her mother and, as far as I am concerned, perfected every recipe. Like my mother, she was someone who could well have been a very successful professional chef had she so chosen or had she been given the choice. It was very rare not to see her in the kitchen preparing some dish or another. If she was not in her kitchen, she was in the basement, which was home to an auxiliary kitchen where she often did 'prep work'. It was down there, on an old yellow and green enamel-topped table, that she would make her light-as-a-feather, soft-as-a-baby's-bottom pizza dough. On the gas stove (perilously unventilated), she would prepare sauce or boil pasta for large gatherings that were held there if the main kitchen was unable to accommodate the ever-growing extended family.

That basement to me was a wonderful kind of time capsule and sanctuary. Divided by a staircase that led to an upstairs hallway, it boasted the makeshift auxiliary kitchen on one side (complete with an old washing machine with hand-cranked rollers that was still very much in use) as well as my grandfather Vincenzo's workshop on the opposite side. Along one wall sat a long workbench with ageing hand tools and dozens of glass jars filled with screws, nails, washers, nuts and bolts hanging from their lids, which were nailed to the underside of a wooden shelf. A most sculptural presentation of a handyman's bric-a-brac if ever there was one. In the far-left corner of this space was a door to the room that I loved most: the wine cellar.

This was a low-ceilinged, cavelike room, approximately eight feet by ten feet, that one entered through a roughly made whitewashed door that was rotting from the bottom up due to the excessive dampness to which the floor and walls clung so dearly. Inside to the right were rough-hewn shelves on which rested the countless long-necked soda bottles that held the precious homemade tomato sauce of the last season. I will digress here to explain of what this vital red liquor was composed and how it was made.

Tropiano Bottled Tomato Sauce

– INGREDIENTS –

Bushels of tomatoes (you decide how many)

Salt

Fresh basil

– EQUIPMENT –

One outdoor open fireplace or fire pit, with heavy metal grates

Fire

Two large galvanized aluminium tubs

One white pillowcase

Lots of old long-necked glass soda bottles

One ladle

One funnel

Lots of new soda bottle caps

One bottle-capping device

One thick piece of oilcloth big enough to cover one of the tubs

Enough water to fill one of the tubs

• Make the fire.

• Fill one tub with water and place it on the grate over the fire.

• Take a lot of the tomatoes, shove them into the pillowcase, and squeeze the s#*! out of them over one of the tubs so that the juice of the tomatoes oozes through the weave of the pillowcase, making it look like a relic of the Saint Valentine's Day Massacre. Continue until all the tomatoes are gone or until you feel like Macbeth at the end of his play.

- One by one, fill the bottles (with ladle, via funnel) with the tomato juice and add a pinch of salt and a basil leaf to each.

- Cap the bottles.

- Put the bottles in the water that's in the other tub.

- Cover them with the oilcloth.

- Boil them for a while. (I can't remember what the health ruling is on this so/and/but I take no responsibility for any food-borne illnesses.)

- Take out the bottles.

- Let them cool.

- Put them in my grandfather's wine cellar, or store in a cool, dry place more convenient for you.

This sauce was used throughout the year. It was light and sweet and could be cooked with olive oil, sautéd garlic and onions or doctored up any which way one chose. One or two long days of work for months of red gold. The bottles would be stored in the wine cellar on wooden shelves alongside mason jars containing pickled green tomatoes, or roasted peppers suspended in olive oil, flavoured with salt and a single clove of garlic. From the wooden beams, over these vacuum-sealed treasures, hung small homemade salami and waxy, pear-shaped bulbs of provolone cheese.

And so now we must return to the wine cellar. Yes, we must return to the must. For the must was all-consuming when one entered the wine cellar. Must and mildew, dank and deep, coated everything, including the aged wine press that stood so proudly in the corner. One was sure that new life forms were breeding from the spores that danced on every surface and consequently one's nostrils and lungs after the first inhale. But the pride that my grandfather took in drawing out his vinified love from the fetid oak barrel into the abraded decanter and presenting it to my father or my uncles (and in later years me and my cousins) made up for any respiratory diseases we were sure to contract. It was an honour to be asked to participate in, or even bear witness to, the ritual in the wine cellar. In fact, I remember being furious when my sisters wanted to tag along, as I saw this as a distinctly male rite of passage. At any rate, those of us lucky enough to be present swelled with pride as the cloudy purple liquor was carried upstairs to the table in its decanter, poured into juice glasses, toasted with, and drunk heartily.

Was it the best wine in the world?

No.

Was it the worst?

Very close.

Did it matter?

No.

It was part of my grandfather, whom we adored, and that made it the sweetest liquid ever to pass our lips.

The house that holds that cellar, that kitchen and those memories was sold long ago, but the flavours and aromas, both tart and sweet, musty and fresh, inhabit my nose, my mouth and my heart to this day.

———

In the backyard of the Tropiano house was a sizeable garden in which my grandparents not only grew every vegetable imaginable but also raised rabbits, chickens and the occasional goat or two, all used to sustain a growing family. This garden and their home were a hub of activities that changed with the seasons but were all ultimately dedicated to what would end up on a plate, from the planting of vegetables and raising of animals to the grafting of branches from one fruit tree on to another, to the repairing of the outdoor fireplace in which the bottles of homemade tomato sauce were boiled in order to pasteurize them. My grandparents had left the extreme poverty of Calabria and, like their forebears, knew nothing but labour. All of that labour was dedicated to survival and creating a life with only the most minimal of creature comforts. Nothing went to waste and luxuries were unheard of. Only what was necessary was . . . well, needed.

In southern Italy even into the early twentieth century, a feudal system was still in place, and most people worked the land for wealthy property owners. America held the promise of jobs, for both men and women, outside of the home, yet for many of them this did not mean that the agricultural and manual skills that were basically part of their DNA would no longer be used after they settled down in a new country. In fact, for a great many the mindset never changed. If you could grow it, raise it, hunt it, cultivate it, build it, or repair it yourself, why buy it or pay someone else to do it? Therefore backyards became microcosms of the land they had abandoned.

If you've ever been to Italy, you'll have noticed gardens and grapevines growing just about anywhere and everywhere, terraced expertly up steep hills, down narrow valleys, on rocky outcroppings, or right next to the Autostrada. The Italians have a gift for cultivating and growing some of the best produce in rather extreme geographical settings. For a mountainous country, the number of vineyards and small farms is extraordinary, as are the quality and variety of what they produce. In Sicily, people are willing to risk everything to live and cultivate some of the best vegetables and wine grapes in the volcanic soil near the still-active Mount Etna. In the region of Campania, just outside of Naples, the rich earth beneath a quivering Vesuvius imparts the incredibly deep, sweet flavour of the San Marzano tomato, again a result of millennia-old volcanic soil.

So when my grandparents set up their home in America, they created not only a very large vegetable garden in the backyard but, when my mother was young, a small farmlet with a couple of goats, chickens, rabbits, and any other animal of reasonable size that was in some way useful or edible. And every bit of those animals that was edible was eaten. When a chicken was roasted, the liver, heart and feet were all prepared according to old family recipes and the carcass used to make soup or stock. The same went for the rabbits, which I know is hard for a lot of people to hear. (As kids, my sisters and I would visit the rabbits in their makeshift hutches that my grandfather had hammered together himself out of scrap lumber and bits of old screen doors. We would feed the rabbits and ask him their names. He'd find a way to avoid the question, as I guess he knew it's always best not to name the thing you're going to kill. But I do remember his intimating that the most plump of the brood was not long for this world.)

The goat, whose milk was drunk straight from the teat by the children, would inevitably be brought to the basement and strung up by its hind legs; its throat would be slit, its body drained of its blood, and finally it would be quartered.

I have it on good authority that when my parents were engaged, my father was present at one of these intimate eviscerations. However, on this occasion, his soon-to-be father-in-law unfortunately chose too dull a knife for the brutal task at hand. Upon witnessing the poor beast suffer so, causing it to urinate all over those present, my father promptly passed out. Seeing her future son-in-law prostrate on the floor, my grandmother turned to her daughter and asked, 'You're going to marry *him*?'

I know it may be disconcerting for many people to hear stories like this, but these events were very much part of everyday life. (Although, why *somebody* didn't sharpen the knife is beyond me.) Even though there was a grocery store a couple of miles away, where of course my grandmother shopped for this and that, old habits are hard to break, especially if there really isn't any need to. The hunting, skinning, quartering, and ultimately eating of all sorts of animals were important traditions to be cherished. I was about thirteen when I entered my grandmother's back porch one day to find her skinning a squirrel given to her by a friend who had gone hunting that day. I was agog. I looked at her as though she were mad and she looked back at me quizzically, as though *I* were the one who was mad. I remember many times opening up the freezer to find neat rows of blackbird corpses in plastic wrap, as well as eels or a variety of venison cuts, all gifts from friends who had recently fished or hunted.

In return for these gifts, my grandmother would offer payment. Obviously it would have been an insult to take money for what was considered a gift, but an offer to pay had to be made, and she always did so. After a short, mostly-for-show squabble about money that shouldn't have been offered and would never be taken, my grandmother would present the gift giver, by way of thanks, with homemade cookies, pizza, a savoury pie or a bottle of my grandfather's wine, all of which were always on hand. I like these little acts of generosity, as I believe they make for deeper friendships, especially if the gifts are something one has made by hand or done something out of the ordinary to acquire.

Speaking about these moments of giving someone you love a practical gift, my parents never visited their parents without bringing something. (I still cannot bear the thought of arriving at someone's home empty-handed.) However, in my family, this simple act was never as cut-and-dried as it should have been.

Let's say that we visit my grandparents on a Sunday and my mother has brought a chicken, some cheese she knows my grandmother likes, and maybe a Fanny Farmer chocolate sampler to satisfy her sweet tooth.

Let's say that happens.

Usually the person receiving the gifts might react with something like, 'Oh, thank you for the chicken and the *blah blah*, but there was no need for you to do that.'

The other person might reply, 'Oh, it's nothing. The chicken was fresh and on sale and I know you like *blah blah*.'

The recipient would then probably say something like, 'Well, that's very generous of you.'

And that would be the end of that. And in most families, that *would* be the end of that.

But, no. No. Not in my family. In fact, very much the *opposite* inevitably happened during a visit to my grandparents of a Sunday. So that you might best understand it, I have dramatized one of these events below. It's important to note that these people all love each other very much.

The Departure

We are in a kitchen in a small working-class home in Verplanck, New York, circa 1972.

Around a long table sit my sister Gina, nine; my sister Christine, six;

me, twelve; my father, forty-three; and my maternal grandfather, seventies. At the sink are my mother, late thirties, and her mother, my grandmother, sixties.

A large meal has just been completed. My grandmother starts to fill a plastic bag with fresh vegetables.

MY MOTHER: What are you doing?

MY GRANDMOTHER: I'm giving you some of the tomatoes.

MY MOTHER: I don't want any.

MY GRANDMOTHER: They're from the garden.

MY MOTHER: I just got some from *Grace's* garden.

MY GRANDMOTHER: How are they?

MY MOTHER: Nice.

MY GRANDMOTHER: Well, take these too.

MY MOTHER: I don't want 'em.

MY GRANDMOTHER: Why not?

MY MOTHER: Because, I already . . . All right, just give me a few.

MY GRANDMOTHER: They're beautiful, look.

MY MOTHER: I see them.

TASTE

My grandmother adds more than a few tomatoes to the bag.

MY MOTHER: What are you doing?

MY GRANDMOTHER: I'm giving you the tomatoes.

MY MOTHER: How many are you giving me?

MY GRANDMOTHER: I don't know.

MY MOTHER: Stop. That's enough.

MY GRANDMOTHER: Just take the tomatoes!

My mother sighs. A silence. The men finish their wine.

MY MOTHER: Kids, get your coats.

We do.

MY MOTHER: (*to my father*) Are you okay to drive?

MY FATHER: Who? Me?

MY MOTHER: Yes, you.

MY FATHER: I'm fine.

MY MOTHER: How much wine did you have?

MY FATHER: Not enough for you to worry about.

MY MOTHER: Have a coffee.

MY FATHER: I *had* a coffee.

MY MOTHER: Then why are you having wine?

MY FATHER: Because your father poured it for me.

MY MOTHER: That doesn't mean you have to drink it.

MY FATHER: Well, it would be impolite.

He looks at my grandfather, who nods and smiles. My father finishes the wine and stands up. My grandmother hands him the now very full bag.

MY GRANDMOTHER: Here.

MY FATHER: Thank you.

MY GRANDMOTHER: And here.

She tries to hand him a five-dollar bill.

MY FATHER: What's that?

MY GRANDMOTHER: Just take it.

MY FATHER: No, for what?

MY GRANDMOTHER: For the chicken you bought.

MY FATHER: I don't want it.

MY GRANDMOTHER: Just . . . !

She stuffs the five dollars into the bag.

MY FATHER: I really don't want it.

He takes it out of the bag. My mother comes over and snatches the five dollars out of his hand. She crumples it into a ball and throws it on to the table.

MY MOTHER: Mom, I don't want it.

MY GRANDMOTHER: Oh, for God's sake.

MY MOTHER: (*looking in the bag*) What the hell did you put in here?

MY GRANDMOTHER: Nothing.

My mother takes the bag and rummages through it, inspecting various items.

MY MOTHER: I don't want any zucchini. I just bought some.

MY GRANDMOTHER: Well, these are good ones.

MY MOTHER: I *bought* good ones.

My mother removes the zucchini.

MY GRANDMOTHER: Just take 'em!

MY MOTHER: I don't *want* 'em!

My mother slams the zucchini on the table.

MY GRANDMOTHER: Ugh, you are so obstinate.

My grandmother discreetly picks up the crumpled five-dollar bill from the table and straightens it.

MY GRANDMOTHER: Where's your son?

ME: (*from the living room*) In here!

MY GRANDMOTHER: Where are you?

I appear.

ME: Right here.

MY GRANDMOTHER: (*sotto voce*) Take this.

She hands me the five-dollar bill.

ME: No. Nonna, I –

MY GRANDMOTHER: Take it.

MY MOTHER: Mom!

MY GRANDMOTHER: Well, let *him* keep it if you don't want it.

ME: I'll keep it.

My father gestures to me to give him the money. I do. He places it on the table next to my grandfather, who gives a slight shrug.

MY MOTHER: (*pulling a hunk of cheese from the bag*) What's this doing in here?

MY GRANDMOTHER: What?

MY MOTHER: This is the cheese I just brought you.

MY GRANDMOTHER: *You* take it.

MY MOTHER: Why would *I* take it? I gave it to you.

MY GRANDMOTHER: Yeah, but you like it.

MY MOTHER: So do *you*. That's why I bought it for you!

MY GRANDMOTHER: I got enough cheese.

My mother opens the refrigerator and literally throws the cheese in and slams the door.

MY MOTHER: Unbelievable. Okay, kids, we're going!

MY GRANDMOTHER: I don't know why you just won't take the money.

MY MOTHER: Because I don't *want* the money. I swear to God I'm never bringing anything to you again.

MY GRANDMOTHER: Good. I don't need anything.

MY MOTHER: Kids!

US: (*from the other room*) We're here!

MY FATHER: Come say goodbye.

My sisters and I enter and say goodbye to our grandparents. As we do my grandmother hands us each a one-dollar bill. Actually, she shoves it down our shirt fronts.

US: No, Nonna, no . . .

MY GRANDMOTHER: Be quiet and take the money or none of you are coming back here again!

We look to our father, who just nods his head and slowly blinks his eyes, which means 'It's okay to take the money.'

US: Thank you, Nonna.

MY GRANDMOTHER: You're welcome. Goodbye.

We kiss her in turn but she doesn't actually kiss back. She offers up a cheek and then bats our lips away with it. My father hugs my grandfather and kisses my grandmother on the cheek. My mother kisses my grandfather.

My mother then kisses my grandmother, meaning their cheeks collide.

MY MOTHER: Okay. Thanks, Mom.

MY GRANDMOTHER: For what?

MY MOTHER: I'll talk to you this week.

MY GRANDMOTHER: If I'm still alive.

My grandfather rolls his eyes. My father smiles.

MY FATHER: Jesus.

We all shout goodbye to each other a few more times as we depart.

On our way out, I see my grandmother return to the kitchen and my grandfather walk to an upholstered rocking chair, take an Italian newspaper from underneath the cushion, sit down, and begin to read.

The house is silent.

———

The Tropiano home not only reaped the benefits of their expertly nurtured garden but was so near the Hudson that my grandparents were able to cull its edible riches as well. As a boy, I loved going to the Hudson River with them, tying pieces of raw chicken to the bottom of crab nets and lowering them off the end of an abandoned steamboat dock into its murky waters.

It's important to note that I have just written that the crabs came from the Hudson River.* Some of you may know that, like most major waterways in our purple-mountained majesty, it is extremely polluted,

---

* Even though in England the variety of crabs is wonderful, for me the cream of the crustaceous crop is the American East Coast blue crab. Sweet, delicate, and just enough flesh to make it worth one's while to keep hammering away at them for hours on end.

or at least, it was at the time.* A General Electric plant upriver released 1.3 million pounds of PCBs (or 'polychlorinated biphenyls', which are used as a coolant in electrical apparatus and, as it turns out, are highly toxic), between 1947 and 1977, into what was once known as 'the Lordly Hudson'. Compounding this ecological indignity, the Indian Point nuclear plant, situated one short mile from my grandparents' home, literally sucked millions and millions of gallons of water from the Hudson to cool its reactors, killing marine life and leaking toxic effluvium into the groundwater that eventually found its way back into the river itself.

Yet unaware of or just choosing to ignore all this, my family ate what the river had to offer, and as far as I know, none of them ever got cancer or even as much as a stomach ache from doing so. One can only chalk this up to the fact that the Italian immune system is staggeringly strong. The Calabrese are known in Italy as '*teste dure*'. Translated literally, it means 'hardheads' and points to an innate stubbornness. However, given the longevity of my family members, it seems that their bodies may be even more stubborn than their minds.

At any rate, after we had spent a few languid hours catching these atomic crabs, they were boiled and dumped unceremoniously on to a table covered in newspaper beneath a pergola wrapped in grapevines in my grandparents' backyard. They were served with corn

---

* Organizations like Riverkeeper have made a significant difference in rectifying this.

on the cob,* boiled potatoes, tomato salad and my grandmother's homemade bread. Obviously there was wine, made by my grandfather, and cold beer, usually Schaefer or Black Label, those inexpensive but thirst-quenching ubiquitous brews of the 1960s and 70s.

If you have ever boiled and eaten a crab yourself, you know that they are a fair amount of work for the small amount of meat they offer. You will also know the gustatory reward is well worth it. Yes, we loved this reward, but perhaps even more, we loved the conversation the laborious process engendered, as well as the excuse it gave us to stay *a tavolo* even longer than usual.

As for the sides, the potatoes were boiled, salted and drizzled with olive oil. The tomato salad was prepared as follows.

---

* Although people often associate corn with the Midwest, New York State has some of the best sweet corn on earth. Come August, grocery stores and farm stands are overflowing with a variety of corn that I believe is called Silver Queen, whose kernels are small and white.

Tomato Salad

— SERVES 4 —

8 small ripe tomatoes (quartered or halved, depending upon their size)
A garlic clove, halved
A glug of extra virgin olive oil
A small handful of basil leaves, torn
A splash of red wine vinegar (optional)
Coarse salt

- Place the cut tomatoes in a bowl with the garlic, olive oil, basil, and vinegar, if using. Toss.

- Salt a few minutes before serving. (Adding it too soon will draw the water out of the tomatoes and dilute the dish.)

The corn on the cob was boiled for about six minutes, placed on a large platter, and brought steaming hot to the table. Greedy hands then grabbed hot ears. But the buttering of the corn . . . well, it wasn't just 'put knife into butter, put butter on corn with knife'.

No.

No.

Good God.

No.

A piece of homemade bread was buttered and then used to

slather the salted ear of corn, thus, in true Italian fashion, creating two dishes out of one, the ear of corn being the first dish and the homemade bread (now saturated with the melted butter, salt and sweetness from the buttered kernels) being the second. This may have been the single most delicious part of an already delicious meal. An act so simple it's almost stupid. But no one I know does it, except my family. And, as far as I know, they are not simple or stupid. (Well, maybe one or two.) I can only suggest that the next time you eat corn on the cob, try the above, and I think you'll taste what I mean.

When the meal and the inevitable game of bocce that followed were over, it was time for us to leave. As we made our way back home and my sisters and I dozed off in the back seat, our car carried the faint aromas of butter and crab as additional and welcome passengers.

3

In 1973 my family moved from our home in Katonah to Italy for a year as my father had taken a sabbatical to study drawing, sculpture and bronze casting at the renowned Accademia di Belle Arti, situated in the heart of Florence. My mother, my sisters and I had never been north of Vermont or south of Manhattan, nor had we ever been on a plane, so the prospect of flying halfway across the world to live in a completely different country, and in a city no less (as opposed to the suburbs), was thrilling and of course a little nervous-making.

When we arrived in Rome, we stayed in a *pensione* for a couple of nights in order to do some sightseeing before taking a train to Florence. We visited the usual places of significance, the Sistine Chapel, the Colosseum, the Roman Forum, etc., which were overwhelming for eyes that had never seen anything older than Rockefeller Center, the Empire State Building, or a few relatives. At the end of each day we ate in a restaurant just a few doors down from where we were staying, and if truth be told, it was the first *actual* restaurant I had ever eaten in. Even though I was almost thirteen years of age, as far as I can recollect, basically the only eatery I had been to was a pizza joint a couple of miles from our house called the Muscoot Tavern.

The Muscoot was named after the reservoir it was adjacent to, one of many reservoirs in upstate New York that supply the drinking water for New York City. Built in the 1920s, it was a narrow, dilapidated shack of a building with a floor that sloped like a perpetually keeling ship. It was dark and dingy, with a battered wooden bar and about twenty checked tablecloth-covered tables. Cold beer on tap, Miller High Life or the like, was served in scratched glass pitchers for about $2 each. Iceberg lettuce salads were served in those small flimsy 'wooden' patchwork bowls that still grace tables in certain diners all over America. However, regardless of the crumbling surroundings and I believe a multitude of health violations, the place did a hearty business, because the thin-crust pizza was delicious. (Many other pizza places opened over the years as that area of upper Westchester became more and more populated, yet none of them ever made pizza that was nearly as good.) My family would go to the Muscoot maybe two or three times a year as a special treat, and besides a hamburger at the Mount Kisco Friendly's after our annual doctor's check-up, that was my experience of dining out. (I recently discovered that Massimo Bottura's wife, Lara Gilmore, waited tables at this very same Friendly's, as she comes from Bedford, New York, next to my hometown of Katonah. I just thought you'd want to know that information and it allowed me to drop Massimo's name, which I will now continue to drop, among others.)

Anyway, fifty years ago there were very few restaurants in that part of Westchester, and those that existed were either diners or very high-end places serving duck *à l'orange* or other French classics that were all the rage in 1970s America. Public school teachers' salaries being what they were, and frankly still are, dining out for a family of five was cost-prohibitive, so logically, we ate in. Also the fact that my mother was such a good cook made it certain that we never would have got anything nearly as delicious as what she was serving on any given night even in the upscale restaurants, and surely not at any of the diners.

So eating in a restaurant, but especially *eating in a restaurant in Rome!!*, was a whole new world for my sisters and me. Do I remember what we ate those two evenings? No, I do not. Most likely, it was just a simple pasta dish that would hopefully satisfy three children aged twelve, nine and six enough to make them sleep through the night and not awaken their exhausted and anxious parents. However, what I *do* remember is the tidiness and cleanliness of the place and that, like most Italian restaurants to this day, it was very brightly lit. I remember how precisely the place settings were laid, that the glasses were turned upside down and then deftly set right by the waiter as we were seated. I remember the starched white tablecloths and how the waiters' jackets were equally starched and white, and I remember how kind they were to us as my father explained with pride, in his then-slightly-broken Italian, that we were to be living here for a year. All that surrounded me was completely alien, and I loved it. I loved the taut readiness of the dining room, the preparedness of the staff, and the sense of expectation that sat invisibly at the empty tables. Who knew what might happen here on this or any given evening?

I don't know why, but I have always been fascinated by and taken great comfort in watching a restaurant being prepped for opening by the staff, their vests or jackets still unbuttoned, bow ties dangling from pockets or draped around necks. I particularly like the moment when the dining room is finally ready and the maître d' unlocks the door, swings it open invitingly, then steps back inside and waits for the first customer to enter as the waiters do up the last buttons on clean and freshly pressed uniforms.

When we returned to Rome many months later, we visited the same restaurant, as my father must have felt a certain loyalty to the place because they had been so welcoming to us as new arrivals. As we sat down he reminded the waiter that we were the same family that had visited some time before. Without missing a beat, the waiter threw up his hands and with a huge smile welcomed us back and even called my sisters by name. How this man, who was no spring chicken, had that kind of memory given the number of people he had waited on since our first visit and over a lifetime, we may never know. All I can say is that he was a testament to the professionalism and innate graciousness of the precious figure that is the Italian waiter.

When we settled in Florence, I did not speak a single word of Italian, so I was enrolled in an Italian school but placed in the year behind where I would have normally been at my age in order to learn proper grammar along with the other students. This proved to be a very wise choice, because within two months I was speaking fluently, and by the end of our stay I was correcting any correspondence that my father had to write in Italian. (Unfortunately, today my Italian is hardly fluent, a result of not speaking it every day. But I have been taking lessons, and frequent trips to Italy have given me opportunities to practise, although I pity the very patient natives with whom I converse.)

Unlike in America, there were no school lunches. School started at around eight thirty and finished at one p.m., at which time everyone went home for the midday meal and an afternoon rest. To compensate for these short hours, we did, however, have classes on Saturday mornings from nine a.m. to twelve p.m. I loved these hours, as they gave me much more free time in the afternoons. Of course, this schedule was conceived with the assumption there would always be an adult at home to care for the children when they arrived for lunch. Today things have changed distinctly, but in the Italy of the early seventies there was always someone, usually a mother or a grandparent, in the household at any given time of the day.

Having an adult present at home consistently was of even greater importance when spring brought warm weather as, purely by coincidence I am sure, during this time teachers' strikes became more frequent. We had experienced a few strikes by the faculty throughout the year, but we were usually told in advance if and when one was pending. What exactly these sudden walkouts pertained to we never knew, but as kids we welcomed them. By the time spring had *fully* arrived, the trees were in blossom, the blue Italian sky floated overhead, and summer was just around the corner, the strikes were even more frequent and came without any forewarning. I remember walking to school a number of times and entering halls that were empty of staff, with the exception of some administrator who would tell those of us milling about looking for some kind of guidance, '*Ragazzi! Non c'è scuola oggi. C'è un sciopero. Tornate a casa!*' ('Kids! There is no school today. There is a strike. Go home!')

And so we would go home. Happily.

When the strikes first began, my mother of course questioned my unexpected return and I would cheerily explain that there was a strike. At first she and my father were shocked. They both worked in an American high school, where nothing like this would ever happen. But eventually, as the teachers absented themselves with more frequency and I regularly reappeared in the apartment a mere half hour after having just left, she would roll her eyes and shake her head.

My sisters were enrolled in a Catholic school, and because nuns are not inclined to protest for better wages or shorter hours, they were schooled consistently. However, for me, although I did learn proper Italian, my schooling in Italy was the best education I almost had.

At this point in the chapter I would write about all the food I ate in Italy over the course of that year, but I am afraid that, unless we were travelling to another city to sightsee or visiting relatives in Calabria, we ate at home. The sabbatical required that my father's salary be reduced for his year abroad, and even though the bygone Italian lira was very weak compared to the American dollar, it still made no sense for our family to dine out. Even when we travelled through the country by train, my parents always bought all the ingredients to make sandwiches as opposed to paying extra to buy them pre-made. This means that not until I began to travel to Italy on my own many years later would I begin to experience the wonder and diversity of native Italian cooking.

Yet there is one meal I remember having during the trip to Calabria. We were in the city of Cittanova, deep inside the toe of the Italian boot, where both my maternal grandparents were born, but only my grandfather still had relatives there. He and my grandmother had come to visit us in Florence, and we all made the pilgrimage to their hometown. Like most of the cities in Calabria and throughout the south, Cittanova was still a very poor place then. My first impression was that I had gone far back in time. Compared to Florence, there were significantly fewer cars, the buildings were crumbling, and most of the inhabitants wore black, as was the tradition south of Rome when a family member had died. But because most families were so large, there was always somebody dying on any given day, so basically everyone just wore black all the time. My relatives all wore black for this reason, but in particular because one of the patriarchs had been killed accidentally in a Mafia shooting. It seems he happened to be in the wrong place at the wrong time, meaning he was walking next to someone who was the target of a hit and he himself caught the better part of a shotgun blast. However, I did hear recently that this was a slight whitewashing of the truth. No one will probably ever know for certain what happened, and perhaps it's best that we never do.

Although the streets of Cittanova were very clean, as I said, the majority of the buildings were in disrepair, to put it mildly. People were living in houses that had been built hundreds of years before, many still with hard-packed dirt floors and often no indoor plumbing. The house we stayed in belonged to one of my grandfather's sisters and had tiled floors, but no hot running water. I remember my dad going out to the stone shed in the small back garden and shaving with hot water that had been boiled on the stove because there wasn't even an indoor bathroom. In fact, an indoor toilet had only recently been installed. But only a toilet. No sink.

We stayed in Cittanova for five days, allowing my grandparents to catch up with the family and for us to get to know them. There were my grandfather's two sisters, their children, and then *their* children, plus other cousins and then even more cousins and so on, all of whom lived within a very short walk or drive of one another. I remember being slightly overwhelmed by the amount of my maternal DNA in every room at any given moment.

I don't remember ever leaving the city confines, with the exception of one trip to the mountains. Our relatives decided we were going to have a feast to celebrate our visit, and at the centre of this feast would be a goat. A couple of the men asked my dad if he wanted to join them on the drive to buy the goat, and he asked if I wanted to tag along. As I was in a very hot city where there was little for a boy my age to do, I jumped at the chance. We hopped in a car and drove about forty minutes up into the Calabrian mountains. It is a harsh landscape but cultivated wherever possible by its resourceful inhabitants. I had never seen land so dry, so coarse, so stubbornly beautiful. But perhaps the highlight for me was that every few miles we would pass a pillbox still standing since the war that had ended almost thirty years before. As a World War II obsessive, I was agog and my heart began to race as I pictured Allied troops battling it out with their Axis counterparts on the very land that surrounded me. Even now, almost eighty years since the end of the war, Italy still has a great number of pillboxes that remain intact, particularly on the coasts of Sicily, Sardinia and the mainland's southern shores. Like so many things that have been discarded or are disused, in the poorer parts of the world, the pillboxes are put to practical use. In Sardinia I have seen them used for storage by seaside restaurateurs or as a shed for a local farmer, and in Sicily as a night-time retreat for teenagers looking for privacy to do whatever teenagers do in private, which in every country always includes tatty blankets, cheap alcohol and condoms. Not that any of us would know.

We arrived at a small hut at the top of a mountain from which one could see across all of Calabria from the Tyrrhenian Sea to the Ionian, or so it seemed. We met the goatherd, who was an old man dressed as though he were out of a children's storybook, complete with thick woollen trousers, a corduroy coat and a felt hat. After a few minutes money was exchanged (my father insisted on chipping in but his attempts were shooed away by his in-laws); the skinned, gutted and cleaned carcass of a goat was placed into the trunk of the car; and we made our descent back towards Cittanova.

Unfortunately, I was not privy to the preparation of the goat, but I remember sitting down at the long table with these new-found great-aunts, uncles, and second and third cousins, all of whom were thrilled that we were visiting and made us feel so welcome. They talked animatedly over one another in the Calabrese dialect, which was practically indecipherable to me even though by then I spoke Italian very well. They passed around bottles of wine; told jokes; offered '*brindisi*', spontaneous rhyming toasts in honour of beloved guests; and of course devoured the goat, which was delicious.

I remember thinking, as I looked around the table, that I had never seen my grandfather so happy. He was back home after many years, among people he loved in a culture that was his. I wondered what it would have been like for him to leave his home so many years ago knowing that he might not return for a very long time, or, when or *if* he ever did return, how many of his loved ones would still be there. He had been raised here, been conscripted into the Italian army during the First World War, and seen action in the brutal battles in the mountains of northern Italy, only to come back home to a poverty that precipitated his leaving to find a better life in America. I cannot to this day fathom that life. What he had to do to survive, to move steadily forward as the world changed so rapidly around him and its leaders continued to make the same mistakes over and over again. Like many Italian immigrants of that era, the life he led was a very simple one. A family, a steady job and a garden were the bastions that tethered him firmly to this world and protected him from the swift swirling chaos of the twentieth century.

There is only one other strong gustatory reminder of my year in Italy. It's a snack for which I was given a bit of pocket change every day after school, known as *schiacciata*.

Schiacciata is the Tuscan version of *focaccia*. It's basically made in the same way but it is '*schiacciata*', meaning it is smashed, therefore making it thinner. After being rolled out, the dough is 'smashed', or pressed down with one's fingers, creating little craters in the surface, before being drizzled with olive oil, sprinkled with lots of coarse salt, and then baked. The result is a crispy crust and a slightly soft but not fluffy or doughy interior. Every day outside my school, a vendor sold from a cart what was basically a mass-produced version of *schiacciata*, slathered in oil and coated with excessive amounts of salt in little wax-paper envelopes, to groups of ravenous young teens who forked over a precious one hundred lire. As cheap as it was in every way, still to this day, whenever I eat a *schiacciata*, a *focaccia*, or any other iteration of Italian flatbread, that after-school snack is the gold standard to which they are and will forever be compared.

4

At the end of almost a year abroad, we returned home to Katonah, and I must say, my sisters and I were very happy to be
back. We had missed our friends and all the American things we had
grown up with, particularly on the food front. Although my mother
still cooked healthy meals for us that we loved, it was peanut butter
and jelly sandwiches, the occasional Swanson TV dinner on a Saturday night, a Velveeta sandwich, or frozen Buitoni 'pizzas' that we had
been longing for.

Given the availability of products from just about anywhere in
today's global market, it seems absurd, but in 1970s Italy, peanut butter was basically non-existent. For Gina, Christine and me, this was
outrageous and unfair. We *loved* peanut butter. We ate it almost every
day. Peanut butter with jelly, jam, honey, bananas, Marshmallow
Fluff or BUTTER, slathered on pieces of extremely white bread or a
crusty Italian loaf. In fact, when an aunt and uncle came to visit us
while we were in Florence, per our desperate request, they brought a

small plastic vat of peanut butter, which my sisters and I fought over for weeks until we had scraped the vessel dry. Peanut butter is not really bad for you, but our other food obsessions, like Velveeta and Buitoni pizzas, were of little or no nutritional value.

For those not 'in the know', Buitoni frozen pizzas are (or *were*; do they still make them? Actually they do) little discs of dough filled with a paste that is supposed to be tomato sauce with dried herbs and cheese. These frigid pucks were taken straight from the freezer and slipped into the toaster, then into one's mouth. In essence they were a savoury Italianesque version of a Pop-Tart. And we loved them. Why, you ask? They were the opposite of our normal fare. They were like the occasional Swanson TV dinner or the slab of Velveeta on white bread with mayonnaise. They were what our friends ate, and so we coveted them. In hindsight this is obviously the reason my mother bought all of these things for us even though they were anathema to her. Yes, they were quick and easy snack foods with which to placate us, but I'd like to think that she bought them so we might feel like we 'belonged'. However, it is more than likely that they ended up in our fridge so we would stop constantly haranguing the poor woman to buy them.

With that preface, here is a glimpse into what I ate as a teenager on any given day during the school week.

Breakfast: *Two or three bowls of cereal with milk, Rice Krispies or similar; two pieces of toast with butter and jam or jelly (usually Welch's grape jelly, which is really like sweet purple aspic); some orange juice.*

Lunch: *Three peanut butter and jelly sandwiches on white bread, usually Wonder, or half a loaf of Italian bread filled with veal cutlets, eggplant parmigiana, or whatever was left over from the previous night's dinner; a piece of fruit; a packaged store-bought sweet – Twinkies or the like.*

After-school snack: *One or two American cheese or Velveeta (is it still made legally?) sandwiches on white bread with mayonnaise, or three or four open-faced peanut butter sandwiches, often layered with sliced banana; a few glasses of milk; another packaged sweet; some fruit.*

Dinner: *Two or three bowls of pasta and three or four chicken or veal cutlets, or two pork chops, or two helpings of London broil (I have only ever seen this cut of beef in America. Never in London. I must find out where it got its moniker), or a lot of whatever other entrée my mother made; vegetables; green salad; dessert.*

Late-night snack: *Two of any of the aforementioned sandwiches, or a large bowl of leftover pasta, or any of the leftover entrées, probably sandwiched between two pieces of Italian bread.*

If a dietician were to count the number of calories ingested and some of their questionable sources, they would be more than concerned for the person who dared consume them. Were they obese, diabetic, depressed? No. It was I. I was very slim, was athletic, had boundless energy, and was always hungry. I did, however, suffer with stomach issues ever since birth, and this kind of diet exacerbated them as the years went by.

My Stomach

Finally, at the end of my twenties, I discovered I was lactose intolerant and also could not digest sugar very well. I forthwith removed both from my diet and luckily saw some improvement, but still problems persisted. In short, I suffered from constant bloating and IBS-like symptoms.

I know this might seem like TMI, but if you are a food obsessive and, due to allergies or a faulty digestive system, eating becomes a daily struggle, then everything else in life can be a bit of a struggle as well, especially as we age. It is proven that our guts are inextricably linked to our brains and hence our moods. If our guts are not functioning properly, then we cannot function properly. I had made attempts at going gluten-free for periods of time and found it disheartening, something I did not feel with lactose or sugar. I tried countless numbers of gluten-free pasta, most of which did not even resemble what I knew of as pasta. Others came closer. Rummo, in particular, is for me the one brand of gluten-free pasta that is able to achieve some of the elasticity and depth that we recognize in regular pasta. But otherwise, in place of my favourite addiction (besides exercise, Martinis and Marx Brothers movies), I ended up making risotto more often than not, or gnocchi, because they are made of mostly potatoes with a minimal amount of flour. Buckwheat pasta was also an alternative, but, as it has no gluten at all, it really needs to be made with about 40 to 50 per cent white flour in order for it not to become just brittle, bitter strands that instantly fall apart. (That said, I love thin, pure buckwheat soba noodles, but in an appropriate broth that complements them.) But the really crucial thing is, although they are all viable and tasty options, pasta made from buckwheat, quinoa, corn, rice, lentils, chickpeas, sawdust, or any combination thereof, just doesn't pair up very well at all with most classic Italian sauces. The beauty of pasta made with semolina, soft or durum wheat flour is that there are myriad sauces that will complement it. Tragically it is indeed the *goddamn* gluten that makes the pasta taste so good and function so well when served with something so guileless as butter and cheese or as complex as a slow-cooked meat sauce. Unfortunately this is an undeniable truth, an absolute, like 'The earth is round,' 'I will never grow any taller,' or 'We are all going to die some day.' Therefore, I don't want an impostor! I want *pasta*! Real, actual wheat *pasta*! Perhaps some day a pill will be available to cure the scourge of gluten intolerance. Or just intolerance.

―――――

However, after that little tantrum, I feel it must be said that not all wheat flour pasta works with all sauces. The *shape* of the pasta is as important as the makeup and quality of its ingredients when it comes to the success of pairing it with the appropriate sauce; you might call it a divine coupling.

Italians are very, very, very particular about what pasta goes with what sauce. Only certain '*salse*' complement certain '*paste*' and vice versa. This is why in any worthwhile Italian cookbook there will be at *most* three different types of pasta suggested to accompany a specific sauce. There have been times when someone in my household (no names) made a traditional family sauce and served it with a completely incompatible pasta. I cannot describe the feeling I have when confronted with this. First, I am angry at myself for not being able to cook the meal, most likely because I was doing something annoying like acting (an activity that frankly is beginning to wear a bit thin as the years go by), and second, I am confounded that whoever made the choice (no names) does not innately know that, as per example, the combination of star pasta and a meat *ragù* is an act of heresy. As far as I am concerned they may as well have just cut out my tongue with a broadsword and danced on the graves of my ancestors. Of course, this reaction is extreme and completely unfair. How could they possibly know the finer points of pasta/sauce pairings unless they were raised by an Italian or a food freak? However, when this happens, I take a deep breath, quietly suggest a more appropriate coupling next time (although I vow to myself that there will be no next time because I will be present to stop it), and try not to pity them because they were raised by philistines.

My suggestion to anyone who eats pasta either with or without gluten is, please pair it with the appropriate sauce and vice versa, because you never know who might be watching. Here are a few wonderful and, for me, *acceptable* combinations of *paste* and *salse.*

> Spaghetti: *Salsa pomodoro con tonno*, carbonara, *vongole*
> Rigatoni: Beef-based *ragù*, *all'amatriciana*
> Ditali: *Salsa pomodoro con piselli, salsa pomodoro con cozze*

To bring greater clarity to this subject of pairing appropriately, or to simply obsess a little more about the mating of sauce and pasta, I would like to share some thoughts on '*ragù*'.

Ragù: What, Why, How?

In French cuisine a stew made of vegetables, tomato, and sometimes meat is known as ragout. By all accounts it was the French who brought ragout to Italy, hence the Italianized word '*ragù*'. According to the writer Massimo Lanari, *ragù* was only served as a main dish and not actually used on pasta until the 1800s. It was only then that it became a sauce that always contains some kind of meat and was paired with specific shapes of either fresh or dried pasta.

In England, before chefs like Ruth Rogers, Antonio Carluccio, Gennaro Contaldo and Contaldo's protégé Jamie Oliver introduced the Brits to the depths of the Italian kitchen, spaghetti Bolognese, or 'spag bol', as they call it, was basically the only Italian food besides pizza that was eaten throughout their green and pleasant land. But in Italy you will be hard-pressed to find such a thing as spaghetti Bolognese. This is ironic because the pairing of the spaghetti from the southern kingdom of Naples and *ragù alla Bolognese* from the north was created as a culinary symbol of unification after Garibaldi united Italy in 1861. However, today, were that original pairing ever to transpire on any part of the peninsula, *especially* in Bologna, the cook would be outcast, and possibly be-handed. Today, *ragù alla Bolognese* is traditionally eaten ('traditionally eaten' in Italy means that if you eat it any other way, you will probably end up on a watch list) with fresh pasta like tagliatelle or maybe, *maybe* fettucine. (Although in Naples, paccheri is acceptable, I am told.) The reason for this is that the richness of the sauce needs a pasta of suitable shape and texture to absorb it properly. Dried spaghetti does not hold *ragù alla Bolognese* in this way and is therefore frowned upon as an appropriate pairing. I have spoken to the great chef and altruist Massimo Bottura about this. He takes this pairing as a personal and cultural affront. Having tried both versions, I happen to agree. I have also eaten Massimo's hand-chopped silky *ragù alla Bolognese* with his handmade pasta and it defies description. (Yes, I will shamelessly continue to brag like this throughout the book.)

Regarding the sauce itself, it is important to know that the Bolognese don't call their meat sauce Bolognese sauce. They call it simply *ragù*. Outside of Bologna it will be known as Bolognese or *alla Bolognese* to differentiate it from other meat-based tomato sauces. And there are countless variations: with or without tomato; only minced veal; only minced beef; a combination of minced pork, beef and veal; a glug of cream; and so on.

However, having spoken to historians and cooked with a chef at the Artusi Museum in Emilia-Romagna, I can say that the *truest ragù alla Bolognese* recipe is in the brilliant cookbook *Science in the Kitchen and the Art of Eating Well*. This unique tome, published in 1891, was the work of Pellegrino Artusi, a seventy-one-year-old retired businessman who was the first person ever to assemble hundreds of recipes from every region of Italy and put them into a single cook-book. Originally containing 450 recipes, it now contains over 700 and is like a second Bible in the home of most Italians.

Artusi's recipe is a mixture of salted pork, ground veal, carrots, onions, celery, stock, salt, butter, nutmeg and a pinch of flour; has no tomato at all; and is cooked in about ten minutes. It was originally sug-gested that it be served with denti di cavallo (horse teeth) pasta, which I had never heard of and sounds very unappetizing, but today it is primarily served with fresh tagliatelle. Artusi's method is purported to be the most authentic way of preparing this now-world-famous sauce and the basis of the countless varieties we eat today.

Other *ragù* use no ground meat but are simply slow-cooked meat-*based* sauces. Many Italian Americans call a meat-based *ragù* by the incredibly vague name of 'red sauce' or even 'gravy'. (Gravy to me is what you pour over turkey on Thanksgiving Day.) How those words came to be used I do not know, but their lack of specificity points to the homogenization of Italian cooking by Americans and second- and third-generation Italian Americans themselves. In my household, almost every sauce had a different name, as they were each completely different sauces. On any given day we would eat *salsa Maria Rosa*, marinara, tomato sauce with peas, or a light tomato sauce similar to marinara without oregano, but cooked in a covered pot and not in an open pan like marinara. However, our *ragù* were *alla Bolognese* or my father's family's *ragù*.

It is this latter *ragù* recipe that was brought to America by my paternal grandfather's family and was served every Sunday in my home growing up. Although meat-based and slow-cooked, it is still quite soft and delicate as well as being a very hearty and comforting meal. The base is created with different cuts of meat, such as beef shin, short ribs and pork ribs, all still on the bone, or even a pig's foot, and browned slightly in oil. Meatballs made with ground beef, bread, garlic, parsley, egg and Parmigiano are fried and set aside with the browned meat.* A tomato sauce is slowly cooked for a bit, then the meat and its juices are added, and a short while afterwards, the meat-balls and their juices are incorporated. Like most stews or *ragù*, it is best cooked the day before or early that morning and set aside to allow the flavours to gel. It is served with dried pasta, usually rigatoni, ziti rigati or penne rigate. The reason for using pasta such as these is that the '*rigati*' or 'corrugated' surfaces of ziti or penne hold the sauce much better than the smooth surfaces of their regular versions. (If I were to serve this with fresh pasta, I would use something like gar-ganelli. These are corrugated tubular pasta made by rolling a square of dough around a pencil-sized dowel from one corner to another over a small ridged wooden paddle.)

When the pasta is ready, the meat and the meatballs are removed from the sauce and set on a separate platter. The sauce is strained to

---

* Regarding the meatball, I would say that the key to a great one is good ground beef with a fair amount of fat, mixed with an almost one-to-one meat/bread ratio. The bread should be stale Italian or French white, crusts removed, soaked in water, and strained. Meatballs should actually be renamed 'meat-bread balls' or 'breatballs' – or something like that but not as stupid – as the proper ratio of both ingredients is the key to their success according to this palate.

ensure there are no rogue bone fragments and a ladleful is incorporated into the strained pasta, the rest being poured into a serving bowl, which can be added to each individual serving. The pasta is presented as a first course and sprinkled with grated Parmigiano, or grated Pecorino Romano if your preference is the same as my paternal grandfather's. The meat, which is now so soft it is falling off the bone, and the meatballs are served as a second course on a plate. *Never* are the pasta and the protein served together in this case. Were I to ever place a meatball in my pasta bowl (they were so good I couldn't wait to get at them), I would be roundly chastised by my parents. I was not only ruining the intended flow of the meal but it was considered crass, not unlike eating bread with pasta. Meat, unless it is actually a part of the sauce, as with *ragù alla Bolognese*, is meant to be served separately, just as bread is meant to be eaten *after* pasta and only used as a '*scarpetto*' (meaning, in essence, 'little shoe') to mop up any excess sauce left in the bowl. These are the rules that have existed for generations, and I am happy to abide by them as they make sense. Yes, I know there is a difference between dogma and 'just the way things are because they should be that way' (which is also sort of the definition of dogma, I think), but the line between the two is thread thin when it comes to certain things culinary in my family.

It was the aroma of this *ragù* that I awakened to practically every Sunday morning of my childhood. Even today, when I am with my parents on a Sunday, it is this traditional meal that we share.

Here is the recipe for the Tucci family *ragù*.

Ragù Tucci

This is the traditional way the Tuccis make *ragù*. My maternal grandmother made a lighter version of this same sauce. It calls for spareribs and stewing beef in this recipe, but different cuts of meat may be added depending on what is on hand – pork chops, sausage, pig's feet. It is delicious with *polpette* (meatballs), which may be added to the sauce during the last half hour of cooking. The sauce may be prepared two days ahead of serving. Refrigerate it overnight and reheat before tossing with the pasta. It may also be frozen with the meat and meatballs.

– SERVES 8 –

50ml olive oil
500g stewing beef, trimmed of fat, rinsed, patted dry, and cut into medium size pieces
500g country-style spareribs, trimmed of fat, cut in half, rinsed, and patted dry
115g onions, roughly chopped
3 garlic cloves, roughly chopped
125ml dry red wine
175g tomato purée
375ml warm water, plus more as needed
Five 400g cans of whole plum tomatoes, passed through a food mill or puréed in the blender

3 fresh basil leaves

1 tablespoon fresh oregano leaves, chopped, or 1 teaspoon dried

- Warm the olive oil in a stew pot set over a medium-high heat. Sear the stewing beef until brown on all sides, about 10 minutes. Remove from the pot and set aside in a bowl. Add the spareribs to the pot and sear until they are brown on all sides, about 10 minutes. Remove the ribs and set aside in the bowl with the stewing beef. (If your pot is big enough to hold all the meat in a single layer, it may be cooked at the same time.)

- Stir the onions and garlic into the pot. Reduce the heat to low and cook until the onions begin to soften and lose their shape, about 5 minutes. Stir in the wine, scraping the bottom of the pot clean. Add the tomato purée. Pour 125ml of the warm water into the tin to loosen any residual paste and then pour the water into the pot. Cook to warm the paste through, about 2 minutes. Add the tomatoes, along with the remaining 250ml of warm water. Stir in the basil and oregano. Cover with the lid slightly askew and simmer to sweeten the tomatoes, about 30 minutes.

- Return the meat to the pot along with any juices that have accumulated in the bowl. Cover with the lid slightly askew and simmer, stirring frequently, until the meat is very tender and the tomatoes are cooked, about 2 hours. Warm water may be added to the sauce, in 125ml portions, if the sauce becomes too thick. (If you have made meatballs, they may be added during the last half hour of cooking. The meatballs will soften and absorb some of the sauce.)

———

Since expressing those peeves of mine regarding pasta shapes and what sauces they should be coupled with was so satisfying, I am inclined to confess my feelings about another, even more egregious, culinary crime that I have witnessed from time to time. It is the act . . . (*I feel my blood pressure rising as I type. Jesus. I hope I make it through this without having a mini stroke or worse*) . . . the act . . . (*Fuck, I'm starting to sweat*) . . . the act . . . (*Breathe, breathe*) . . . of a full-grown adult . . . cutting their spaghetti!!!!!!!!

When I am privy to this act of sacrilege, in that instant, no matter how charming, intelligent, kind or altruistic the perpetrator is, some of me will hate most of them forever. I will stare, aghast, and sigh, knowing that there is nothing for it. As David Mamet wrote in his great play *American Buffalo*, 'The only way to teach these people is to kill them.'

However . . . breaking *dry* spaghetti, *then* cooking it and using it for certain recipes is welcomed.

Why?

I have no answer for you except, as I say to my children, 'because I said so'. (Or really, it's what my grandmother did and it worked, so I do it.)

Try this recipe below and you will see what I mean. It is my derivation of a recipe I grew up with. I often make a big pot and eat it over a few days for lunch at home or bring it to film sets as an antidote to the usually horrid food served off a truck to cast and crew by beleaguered caterers.

Spaghetti with Lentils

— SERVES 4 —

½ a carrot, finely chopped
½ an onion, finely chopped
½ a stalk of celery, finely chopped
½ a garlic clove, sliced
3 tablespoons extra virgin olive oil, plus more for drizzling
165g dried brown lentils, rinsed and picked over
250g spaghetti
375g marinara sauce
Salt
Freshly ground black pepper

- In a medium or large saucepan (all the ingredients, including the pasta, will end up in this saucepan, so make sure it is large enough), sauté the carrot, onion, celery and garlic in the olive oil over a medium-low heat until they are soft, about 7 minutes.

- Place the lentils in another medium saucepan. Fill the pan with cold water to a level 2cm above the lentils. Slowly bring to a simmer and cook until the lentils are just tender, about 20 minutes. Remove from the heat and set aside.

- To break the spaghetti, lay out a clean dish towel, wrap the spaghetti in it, and fold over the ends of the towel. Roll, squeeze, and/or bend this bundle until you can feel the spaghetti has broken down into 2–4cm pieces. Place the bundle over a large bowl and unfurl, thus emptying it of all the bits of spaghetti.

- Bring a large pot of salted water to a boil. Cook the spaghetti until al dente.

- Reserve half a cupful of the cooking water before draining the pasta.

- Meanwhile, drain the lentils and transfer them to the saucepan with the sautéd vegetables. Add the marinara sauce. Bring to a simmer, cover, and cook until the lentils have blended with the sauce, about 10 minutes. Add the drained pasta, along with the reserved pasta water, to make a liquid consistency. Season with salt and pepper as desired. Simmer the pasta and sauce together to allow the flavours to combine, about 3 minutes. Serve immediately.

5

I moved to New York City after graduating college and into my first apartment on 76th Street between Broadway and West End Avenue in 1982. The neighbourhood, known as the Upper West Side, stretches from 59th Street, south of Lincoln Center, to 110th Street, and from Riverside Drive to Central Park West, both of which, like the smaller cross streets, are purely residential. Running parallel to the latter two north–south streets are West End Avenue (also only residential), Broadway, Amsterdam Avenue and Columbus Avenue. It is on these last three streets where shops, restaurants, gyms and other places of business occupy the ground floor of countless apartment buildings. For generations the Upper West Side was home to a great many Jewish families, and the number of Jewish delis and bakeries was proof of that. It was also inhabited by mostly working- and middle-class families as well as gaggles of actors (particularly those who worked in the theatre, as the Great White Way was at most a thirty-minute walk downtown), many of whom resided in large rent-controlled apartments. I had a small one-bedroom apartment on the first floor and I shared the space and the $660-a-month rent with my girlfriend at the time and a college friend of ours. (Yes, we all slept in the same bedroom. That's bed*room*, not bed.) The place had a living area off which there were a tiny galley kitchen and a small bathroom, neither of which had been updated since the mid-sixties, and the aforementioned bedroom. The living and kitchen area received no natural light at all as its large window overlooked an air-shaft. To make matters worse, this window was protected by an accordion safety gate, making the space feel even more oppressive. The bedroom looked on to the backs of the apartment buildings on 75th Street, and although it received lots of lovely natural light, because of its proximity to the ground floor, it too had a safety gate. So basically, apartment 2D at 107 West 76th Street was like a large prison cell for the three of us in which we could barely afford to incarcerate ourselves.

Eventually our college friend moved out, and soon afterwards my girlfriend and I split up and I was left there on my own. I rather liked living alone at that time, until I went through a long stint of unemployment and was unable to afford the rent one month, which had risen to over $750. I had been receiving unemployment cheques of around $170 a week and painting apartments whenever I could for cash. But this particular month had been a bad one and I was strapped for dough. Refusing to ask anyone for money, I made my way to the Actors' Equity offices and applied for money from the Actors Fund, which a colleague told me I had a right to do. It was not a loan. It was money available to union actors who were struggling to make ends meet. All you needed to prove was that you were a member in good standing and that you had participated in Equity productions fairly consistently. I was told to bring playbills of shows I had been in and reviews of performances as proof of my past employment. The whole idea made me sick to my stomach, but I was desperate. I was too prideful to ask my parents for money even though I know they would have given it to me happily. I knew that the next month I was to start a job and money would be coming in; however, this month I had no other option but to swallow my dignity and go begging, as it were.

The Actors' Equity office was appropriately located in Times Square, the hub of Broadway. I showed the kind fellow behind the desk the necessary documents and he approved the funds straight away. I was extremely embarrassed and humbled but very relieved. I thanked him profusely, and as I stood up to leave he asked me if I needed any shoes.

'Shoes?' I asked.

'Yes, shoes,' he said.

'Um, no. Why?'

'Because you are entitled to a pair, if you need them,' he said softly.

'Oh, um, well, no, I don't. But thank you.'

He nodded and smiled, and I left.

Later, I discovered that this offer of free footwear was a remnant of a time when people basically had one pair of shoes that they wore every day. If you were an actor walking from audition to audition day in and day out trying to get a job, you may well have worn out your shoes in doing so and might have been in need of a new pair, so the Actors Fund had instituted this policy. I don't know if the offer is still made, but I find its thoughtful practicality incredibly moving. A few years later, when I started to make a little money consistently, I made a donation to the Actors Fund of double the amount that had been given me. The Actors Fund is a wonderful and necessary thing that helps Equity members through hard times and in their dotage. If ever you attend a Broadway show at the end of which the cast asks the audience for a donation, please give generously. You never know, a performer you may come to admire in the future might not be able to pay their rent today.

During those couple of years alone in my small apartment, I would cook very simple meals for myself but I was not yet really as interested in cooking as I am today. I mostly made pasta marinara, chicken cutlets and the like. I don't ever remember even using the oven. I cooked everything on the narrow four-burner gas stove. When I didn't cook, I mostly ate in coffee shops, burger joints or Cuban-Chinese places. (I will address the latter in a moment.)

At coffee shops, like John's on 67th Street, whose walls and cabinets still retained the original white enamel of the 1930s, one could order a breakfast of fried eggs, corned beef hash, toast, home fries, orange juice, and a bottomless cup of coffee for about three dollars. For lunch, at the Cherry Restaurant – which was really a glorified Asian-owned coffee shop that also had a full Chinese menu – a soup and a sandwich, like a bowl of split pea and a grilled cheese or a turkey club, was filling and affordable. Dinner out was usually at a burger joint like Big Nick's, which sold enormous, greasy, bloody burgers on plump buns that to this day I still salivate over. (I am actually salivating as I write this just thinking about the goddamn things.) After that heart-stopping repast, either alone or with friends, I would take in a movie for about two bucks or pay a visit to the bowling alley on 76th and Amsterdam that had remained miraculously unchanged since the 1940s. Here I would drink Budweiser or Miller High Life beer from long-neck bottles; eat American cheese sandwiches on white bread, though I had just eaten practically half a cow an hour earlier; bowl the night away; and never spend more than ten pieces of the great bourgeois long green.

Like the West Village, the Upper West Side also had a large gay community, and Amsterdam and Columbus Avenues had many independently owned and operated gay bars and restaurants. Unfortunately, in the mid- and late eighties gentrification took hold, and many buildings were turned into condominiums and co-ops or simply demolished to make way for new, poorly designed dwellings for the up-and-coming at prices that most people could not afford. The skyrocketing rents caused by gentrification also coincided with the AIDS epidemic, forcing many gay-owned businesses to fold just as the disease was taking the lives of many of those who owned them and decimating the ranks of their devoted patrons.

As the profile of the neighbourhood became less diverse in every way, the independent businesses that supported the inhabitants and gave the area its particular flavour went the way of so much of

America and became homogenized. One by one, old coffee shops like John's and the Cherry Restaurant disappeared and were quickly replaced by a Starbucks or some version thereof. Independently owned hardware and clothing stores were replaced by huge chains, as were individually owned pharmacies, shoe stores, bookshops and barbershops, many of the latter with interiors that were unchanged since their heyday of the 1930s and 40s. The beautiful old World War II-era bowling alley was demolished and turned into a cheaply decorated 'upscale' pool hall. What were also lost were many little eateries that reflected the diverse ethnic and cultural profile of the neighbourhood. There were quite a few Jewish delicatessens that served classic dishes like matzo ball soup, potato latkes, pastrami sandwiches (although none nearly as good as those from the now sadly vanished Carnegie Deli) and marble babke. To that point, let us leave the Upper West Side for a moment and head about twenty blocks downtown so I might mourn the loss of the aforementioned Gan Eden of delicatessens.

The Carnegie Deli was founded in 1937 and became an institution beloved by New Yorkers and tourists alike. Usually if any restaurant in any city is discovered and frequented by tourists, native patrons will take their business elsewhere. Yet with the Carnegie Deli this was not the case. Native New Yorkers might have gone at odd hours when the endless line to enter had disappeared and the dining room wasn't so crowded that it became what seemed to me to be a firetrap, but they still went. And the thing is, one couldn't *help* but go there. Yes, the food was good, but it was also a way to get a dose of old New York while too much of the city was making itself brand-new again and again and again. Often, if I had a meeting, had an audition, or was performing on Broadway, I would stop into the Carnegie Deli for a bowl of chicken soup (with noodles *and* matzo balls, thank you very much, I will have both) and a tower of a pastrami sandwich. In every Jewish deli the sandwiches are huge amounts of meat or chicken or tuna salad between two pieces of bread. (Please go on YouTube and find the brilliant comic stylings of Nick Kroll and John Mulaney performing their hilarious sketches in coffee shops revolving around '*too much tuna!*' Your life will be changed for the better.) But the Carnegie Deli took it to the extreme. Their motto was, 'If you've finished your meal, we've done something wrong.' Yet although the sandwiches were monstrous and almost anyone would have been hard-pressed to even get the behemoth of rye and still-warm pastrami in their mouth, let alone finish one, you were not allowed to share a single order. So a friend and I would each order a sandwich, eat as much as we could, and then take the rest to our respective homes for a midnight snack. If I were really peckish I would order the Frisbee-sized latkes with a side of applesauce as well. Waiting for my meal to arrive, I would sip a beer or a cream soda and partake of the pickles floating in the small stainless steel bowl of room-temperature brine that sat on every table. Searching for my catch, I preferred the half-sour pickles; I tried not to think about when the murky liquid had last been refreshed or how many hands prior to mine had fished around for 'just the right one'. On occasion, if I were feeling particularly Chekhovian, I would order the borscht instead of the chicken soup. Any of it was good. All of it was good. The Carnegie Deli's food warmed you up on a frigid February night after you had been to a Broadway theatre or seen a dance performance at City Center just a couple of blustery blocks away. It coated your belly and comforted your soul when you popped in late at night after a few too many at a cheap downtown bar, en route to the one-bedroom apartment you thought you'd be living in for the rest of your life if someone didn't give you a job soon.

But now, like so many wonderful old New York City eateries and bars, the Carnegie Deli is no more. (Okay, to be fair, the reason for the disappearance of the Carnegie is not because the rent was raised or the building was razed. It's because the second-generation owner decided that she had had enough, which is of course her prerogative, but still a terrible loss for all of us.)

However, as I said before, the gentrification of New York has caused many businesses to close that had no desire to do so, as well as the destruction of too many buildings and places of cultural significance to count. (A prime example being the old Penn Station that was brutally razed after its magnificence graced the city for a mere sixty years.) I don't know why, but we Americans feel little obligation to preserve what once *was* because we choose to see it as less than what *is* or what *could be*. Like children and adolescents, we have not yet learned that the present isn't the only thing. Obviously change is good, but there is absolutely no need for us to obliterate the past while creating the future. They can and should live side by side. Wonderful places, some of them very old, like Luchow's, Gage & Tollner and the

Oak Room at the Plaza Hotel, or newer ones, like Elaine's, Kiev and Florent, are now gone. The main reason for their demise is almost always financial. Either the rent is raised, the economy has slumped, the owner would shortsightedly not allow the staff to unionize, or they quite simply went out of vogue. The times and tastes changed but their menus and decor didn't. Had they been able to hang on for a while longer, it is more than likely a new generation would have redis- covered their classic dishes and old-world charm and brought them back to life. Of course there are still a number of old restaurants left around the city, like Delmonico's, Peter Luger, Fraunces Tavern, the Old Homestead and Barbetta, yet considering the physical scope of the city and the fact that there are over 8 million inhabitants, it is a paltry sum. Paris, with 2.2 million people, has dozens.

Who would any of us be if our grandparents and parents had not cherished their familial history and passed it on with reverence in the form of articles of clothing, furniture, china, cutlery, books, photos, artwork, diaries and so on? These mementos don't have to be of great monetary value, only of emotional value. I have pots and pans that were my mother's that I will never part with, not only because 'nobody makes them like that any more' but also because they remind me of her and the extraordinary meals she made for our family. Losing a beloved family heirloom is a very real personal loss; they're things that cannot ever be replaced or re-created. But perhaps the most precious heirlooms are family recipes. Like a physical heirloom, they remind us from whom and where we came and give others, in a bite, the story of another people from another place and another time. Yet unlike a lost physical heirloom, recipes are a part of our history that can be re-created over and over again. The only way they can be lost is if we *choose* to lose them. I know that progress is good for business and business is business, but the careless expurgation of famous eateries and their classic dishes made from historic recipes that helped shape a city is an enormous loss for any culture no matter how you slice it. And if you slice as much of it as a good Jewish deli, particularly as much as the Carnegie once did, then that is a staggering loss indeed.

———

Now let's take a stroll back to the Upper West Side. As we wind our way northward nowadays, we will find that the culinary landscape is quite different from the one I encountered when I first moved there almost forty years ago. Columbus Circle is now home to a monstrous edifice that houses the Mandarin Oriental, a jazz concert hall, offices and apartments as well as an upscale mall and quite a few restaurants. If you have a lot of dough, you can eat at any of them, but only if you've recently robbed a bank will you be able to dine at Per Se, where dinner starts at $355 for a nine-course tasting menu without wine. That's, as I said, *without* wine. Wine is *not included.* There is *no wine pairing* with your tasting menu for $355. Although, if you'd like to save some money and bring your own wine, there is a $150 cork-age fee per bottle. Just beware that a sales tax of 8.875 per cent is also not included. Nor is the wine, as I think I have mentioned. A bargain if ever there was one. I have never eaten there but I hear it's great.

Still heading northward, we pass Jean-Georges Vongerichten's eponymous restaurant in the Trump International Hotel. His restaurant is as wonderful as his landlord is demonic. As we continue up Broadway we see that many rather good but very pricey restaurants have opened in the last two decades alongside chain stores such as the Gap, Brooks Brothers, Pottery Barn and one hundred and seventeen Starbucks. Finally, reaching 78th Street, we come to a fifty-year-old gem of an eatery called La Caridad.

La Caridad is one of the last remaining Cuban-Chinese restaurants in Manhattan. Founded in the late sixties by Rafael Lee, a Chinese immigrant who first went to Cuba and then came to the US, and now run by his son, it is still serving that strange and wonderful mix of Cuban and Chinese dishes at very reasonable prices. If you are not a New Yorker you may well be asking yourself, 'What, why, and how Cuban-Chinese?' The answer is that many Chinese immigrated to Cuba during the mid-1800s to find work building the railroads, and again at the turn of the century and later when Chairman Mao came to power. At the beginning of the Cuban Revolution many Cuban-Chinese fled communism yet again and came to New York. It was here that they opened restaurants serving dishes reflective of their dual ancestry.

My first apartment was a mere two blocks away from La Caridad and therefore I could be found at its tables quite often. There were always at least a few taxis idling on the street outside with drivers eating the restaurant's food from takeaway containers, because like the rest of us they knew that the food was good, the service lightning quick, and the prices absurdly low. The restaurant is almost like a kind of terrarium, as two sides of it are long glass windows looking on to Broadway and 79th Street. Pedestrians love to peer in as they wait at the bus stop just outside the entrance for the downtown Broadway local, just as customers will spend hours at one of the restaurant's tables watching the shirt-sleeved multitude outside bustle through their daily lives. It's a modest-size place that seats about forty people, with no decor to speak of. The staff can be at times brusque but is for the most part friendly in that slightly jaded way that professional waiters are for the most part friendly.

One might order a wonton soup to start, followed by an oxtail stew or shrimp fried rice as an accompaniment to pulled beef in a rich brown sauce, known as *ropa vieja*, all for very affordable prices. Slightly-too-greasy but delicious fried chicken (mostly dark meat) with a side of yellow rice, red or black beans, fried plantains and an avocado-and-onion salad would cost you somewhere between $6 and $8, as I recall. Obviously the prices have increased in the last forty years, but it is still very reasonable. Like other Cuban-Chinese restaurants years ago, it was one of the only places with an espresso machine, and although the coffee was not quite like they make it in Rome, it was a welcome respite from the acidic dishwater that passed for java at most of the coffee shops around. At La Caridad, a large oval plate of shrimp with yellow rice and peas and a side of black beans could sate a young actor for quite a few hours, until he got hungry again and was forced to make himself yet another dinner of pasta marinara washed down with the remains of a cheap bottle of red, because he had spent his allotment of cash for the day. But in his heart of hearts and stomach of stomachs, he knew it had been worth it.

TASTE

Whenever I am in New York I go to the Upper West Side and visit the neighbourhood I was thrilled to be a part of for so many years when I wore a younger man's clothes. As I have said, it has changed distinctly, a bit for the better and a bit for the worse. It is safer and cleaner, but so much of the texture of the past has been lost. I still make a point of eating at La Caridad not only because I love it but because, along with most of my other dining haunts, all the other Cuban-Chinese restaurants within a twenty-block radius have disappeared. Their square footage has been transformed into soulless cafés ruled by tattooed baristas who ask you for your first name so they can write it on your eco-cup and then scream it for all the world to hear when your order is ready. It is in these kinds of places that today one can purchase a cup of coffee for what, when I was young, was once the price of a hearty meal served with an unusual slice of ethnic culinary history on the side.*

---

* While revising this chapter, I discovered that La Caridad closed abruptly on 23 July 2020. I don't know the reason why, but like so many customers, I am heartbroken.

6

After we had been dating for four years, I married my late wife, Kathryn Spath, in 1995. She had two young children at the time. In 2000 we had twins, Nicolo and Isabel, and in 2002 she gave birth to our daughter Camilla. After being diagnosed in 2005 with stage-four breast cancer, she died four years later, in 2009, at the age of forty-seven. She was extraordinary as a mother, wife and friend. She was highly intelligent, beautiful, kind, patient, and one of the best people I will ever know. I loved her and always will. Her death is still incomprehensible to me and her absence still unreal.

Like me, Kate enjoyed good food, as was obvious on our first date in a little French restaurant in Manhattan called Tout Va Bien. It was opened in 1948 and I am happy to say it is still there. We both ordered their always delicious coq au vin, and I think Kate finished hers, half of a baguette, and a couple of glasses of wine before I'd even made a dent in my coq.

When I first met her she was a single mother running a day care centre out of her home to make ends meet. Yet, no matter how tired she was after a gruelling day, she cooked a well-balanced meal and had a proper sit-down dinner with her children every night. The meals were, for the most part, very simple and kid-friendly, but they were varied and nutritious, and subsequently both of her children became very good eaters. When I joined the family, Kate and I naturally started cooking together, and the number and the types of dishes we prepared changed and grew. I introduced my family's recipes into our daily fare and eventually, exactly like my wife Felicity, Kate usually ended up making them better than I did. Some of them *much* better.

I remember one instance not long before she was diagnosed when Kate made my mother's recipe for lasagna Bolognese, a dish that was every family member's favourite. Handmade plain and spinach pasta are layered into a baking dish with Bolognese sauce, *besciamella* and grated Parmigiano. The result is an absurdly rich yet delicate dish that no one who eats it seems to be able to *stop* eating. Needless to say it is very hard to get right. The pasta has to be the correct thickness, just thick enough to hold its shape *and* the sauce but just thin enough to almost melt in your mouth after a single bite. The Bolognese sauce cannot be too meaty, as this would make it too heavy, and it must also have the proper ratio of carrots, celery, onion and tomato to give it the necessary sweetness. The *besciamella* cannot be either too runny or too 'claggy', as they say in Britain, and it must all be put together with great care so as

TASTE

not to damage the sheets of pasta. In short, if you have a lot of time and patience, you should try making it. If you don't, then, really, just don't. You'll make yourself and everyone around you very unhappy.

Kate had been experimenting with this dish for many years and succeeding brilliantly, but would always ask my mother for her opinion or for tips as to how she might improve upon it. My mother is very patient and encouraging when teaching people to cook, but because of her knowledge, experience and prowess she can be a bit intimidating. But Kate as usual was undaunted.

Because of the time-consuming and labour-intensive process of the recipe, it was usually only served on special occasions. One day, just my parents, Kate, my stepdaughter Christine, the little kids and I were celebrating something; what it might have been I can't remember, but it was clearly significant enough for Kate to make this coveted culinary treat. As we all tucked in, it was immediately evident that she had outdone herself. While my dad and I were moaning with delight, I noticed my mother chewing slowly, her eyes fixed in a stare as though she were trying to make the flavours of what she had just put into her mouth permeate every last taste bud. A moment passed, and Kate looked at her and bravely asked, 'What do you think, Joanie?'

My mother continued to chew silently with her eyes still focused on her plate. After a slight, and not un-tense, pause, she looked at Kate and said, 'I have nothing left to teach you.' And then she started to cry.

Kate was beaming as she hugged my mother. The rest of us laughed.

And then we devoured the lasagna.

———————

Eating with my in-laws, Kate's mother, Dorothy, and her second husband, Brad, was a very different experience than when eating with my parents. Although I always enjoyed visiting them, they were not necessarily a couple that liked to cook. Like many people, they enjoyed food but the process of preparing something beyond baked chicken or a steak, or experimenting with new recipes, was of no interest to them. Some people have a penchant for kitchen activities, others don't, but our visits were always enjoyable.

Dorothy and Brad lived in a lovely home on the Maine coast not far from Freeport, an old town now composed mostly of outlet stores such as L.L.Bean and Sebago. Most summers, Kate and I and my stepchildren, and then later, our children, would drive the five hours north from Westchester for a visit. We would go out on their small boat to different islands, take hikes in the woods, or spend hours in the gargantuan L.L.Bean store in Freeport buying things we almost needed, like polar fleeces, thermoses and carabiners. During our stays, inevitably Kate and I would do the cooking, because we knew what our kids would and wouldn't eat, cooking made us happy, and being cooked *for* made my in-laws happy. But there was one meal that Brad made that neither Kate nor I would ever dare attempt.

Brad had been born and bred in Maine and still spoke in the flat tones that 'Mainiacs' are well-known for. For those who have never visited, Maine is a beautifully rugged state with short summers and long, hard winters. Those born in Maine consider anyone *not* born in Maine an 'outsider', no matter how long that person may have lived there. They are for the most part a taciturn folk with a caustic, bone-dry sense of humour. An example of a Maine comic bon mot: Once, trying to make polite conversation at an uptight gathering at a small 'yacht club', I asked a member whether he had lived in Maine his whole life. His reply was a very deadpan, 'Not yet.' The conversation petered out pretty quickly after that.

However, eating lobster plucked from Maine's ever-frigid coastal waters with friends and family is one tradition that seems to scrape the patrician barnacles off even the most stoic of the state's residents. The effort required by everyone at the table to break down and properly dissect a steamed lobster is an act that causes the participants to help one another complete the task. This act removes all barriers and can't help but spark conversation. I have eaten lobster in England, the Maldives, Ireland and many other places, and yet my favourite is still a one-and-a-half-pound lobster from Maine. I am not one who cares for his lobster grilled, Thermidored, or Newburged, however tasty they may be. I am not saying I don't like lobster bisque and don't often crave a lobster roll on a lightly toasted, buttered bun. But when it comes to *fresh* lobster, I think, they are best gently boiled in salted water, and only butter, ideally clarified, is needed to enhance their flavour. This is how Brad cooked them every summer on the beach of a small island off the Maine coast.

On the day of our arrival, Brad would look at the upcoming weather forecast and decide when might be best for our annual island/lobster outing. After breakfast on the chosen day, we would fill coolers with beer, water and soda, hunks of cheese and homemade smoked fish pâté; stuff plastic bags with ears of corn and loaves of bread; gather the lifejackets; and head down to the rocky shore that the house overlooked. In two old burlap sacks, Brad carried a battered and blackened aluminium pot, a small wire shelf from a defunct fridge, and a stash of firewood. We would all then climb into a little dinghy and row to the motorboat moored about fifty yards out. Settled into the boat, we'd head to a nearby marina where there was a lobsterman Brad knew who sold the perfect-size lobsters for a very fair price. Their quick, vicious claws rendered useless by taut rubber bands, the crustaceans were tossed into an empty cooler and whisked on to our boat.

Making our way through the cold blue water towards a small island that had a less rocky beach than most of the other nearby islands, we would pass harems of seals swimming and sunning themselves on the jagged charcoal-coloured rocks. The whole scene was a New England idyll worthy of any Wyeth family member's bristles. We would moor the boat off the island, hop into the dinghy, and row to shore.

I make it all sound simple, but inevitably there was lots of swearing and cursing about mooring lines tied improperly, weight being distributed unevenly, how many trips it would take to get us all ashore, who would go first, and the designated rower's insufferable inability to row in a straight line. However, once we were on the island, tensions were eased by the sound of tabs being hastily pulled on cans of cold beer. Brad and the kids and I would gather stones and pile them in a circle that would contain the fire, while Kate and her mom laid out the hors d'oeuvres. With the logs Brad had brought and some dried pine branches scavenged from the island, we lit a fire, balanced the old fridge grate on the stones above the flames, and waited for it to begin to burn evenly. After a few minutes we filled the aluminium pot with seawater and placed it on the grate over the now-roaring blaze. When the water came to a rolling boil, the lobsters were gently dropped in and covered with seaweed. The sweet corn, just shucked by the kids, was placed on top of the seaweed and then covered with *more* seaweed. Butter was melted in a little pot placed next to the fire while we ate cheese and crackers and waited impatiently for our Maine course. (Pun intended and achieved.)

How Brad knew when the lobsters were ready is beyond me, because he never timed them. It seemed he just knew. And he was never wrong. The meat we pried from the shells was always cooked to perfection. We dipped it greedily into the melted butter and lathered *cold* butter on the hot corn, followed by a sprinkle of salt.

Salt and butter.

Butter and salt.

Those two condiments elevated the flavours of an ancient plant and a prehistoric aquatic decapod to create a staggeringly delicious experience for us all. As I said, this was the only meal Brad ever cooked besides a burger or a steak on the barbecue, but we were all glad that he had directed his energies into perfecting it, because it was extraordinary.

If and when fresh seaweed was at hand, Kate and I always cooked lobster using Brad's fail-safe method, and I pride myself on doing so successfully to this day. However, I'm still not even close to achieving Kate's repeated triumphs with *lasagna alla Bolognese*, but I'm working on it. No doubt Felicity will do so before I've even left the gate.

7

Christmas Eve

Each year, as the days grow shorter in England, where I now make my home, I cannot help but miss the winters of my childhood, appallingly more than a half a century ago, in upper Westchester, New York. Our home on a cul-de-sac at the top of a hill was surrounded by trees, which by early December were almost always laden with snow. The ponds and lakes would begin to freeze over, and the woods around us became studies in hard black and soft white, making them wonderfully mysterious and therefore more inviting than ever. I loved everything about winter, and I loved Christmas in particular. Our Christmases were joyous celebrations that to this day I still attempt to re-create.

Although my parents' funds were limited, they made sure that our house was always elegantly decorated. My father had constructed a modernist manger out of scraps of walnut wood, in which sat contemporary figures of Mary, Joseph and the Christ child. Over the years, other, more traditional store-bought versions of shepherds, wise men and farm animals somehow made their way into our Gropius-inspired stable, but they always seemed to me to be unsophisticated interlopers. Each year, when this homemade '*presepio*' (Italian for 'crèche'), the Christmas tree lights (the large, primary-coloured, hand-painted variety), the stockings, and other decorative holiday bric-a-brac were freed from their crumbling cardboard boxes, I felt an almost overwhelming surge of joy. I knew that Christmas would transport us out of the prescribed, the mundane, and into a week or so of undefined days filled with endless play.

As an Italian Catholic family, though very un-practising, we ate only fish on Christmas Eve. Homemade food from recipes passed down over many generations was our daily fare, but during Christmas this practice was elevated to even greater traditional culinary heights. It's believed that the serving of fish on Christmas Eve comes from the Roman tradition of not eating meat the night before a feast day. In some families this meal is called the Feast of the Seven Fishes, but no one is quite sure why there are seven, other than it is the most used number in the Bible. At any rate, *at least* seven types of fish were served in my home when I was a kid on Christmas Eve. My mother would prepare a meal similar to the one that follows:

Appetizers
Shrimp cocktail
Baked clams
Seafood ceviche

TASTE

Stuffed mushrooms
Zeppole

First course
Salt cod with potatoes, green olives and tomato
Pasta with tuna sauce

Second course
Baked salmon or baked bluefish with breadcrumbs
Roasted potatoes
Green beans
Broccoli di rape
Green salad

Dessert
Ice cream
Biscotti
Apple pie
Panettone
Nuts and dried figs

The above is not an exaggeration. It was also for only five people: my parents, my two sisters and myself. Over the years, with the inevitable addition of spouses, children, friends, etc., the number of dishes stayed the same but the amount of food increased.

Allow me to focus on one dish from each course, beginning with *zeppole. Zeppole*, or 'zeepoli', as they are often pronounced by Italian Americans, are deep-fried, loosely shaped rings or balls of dough made from mashed-up potatoes and wheat flour. (They can also be made with only wheat flour.) When fried in very hot olive oil they instantly puff up and become addictively delicious. Whenever my mother would begin to fry them, the whole family would unconsciously start edging more and more closely to the stove until we were all huddled around her, practically panting with a hunger we didn't know we had until she started cooking. After the *zeppole* have fully puffed and are golden brown, they are plucked out and set aside to cool. As soon as they have cooled enough to handle, they are then devoured by anyone who can grab one the quickest. Because my father had very callused hands from years of sculpting and working with solvents, he was able to snatch the hottest and freshest of the batch. As children we tried to do the same, but it was of no use. Our soft palms and delicate fingertips couldn't handle the heat of those golden, doughy parcels, and we were therefore forced to wait for them to cool as we watched my father try to practically swallow his whole. We did, however, take great comfort in the fact that he would inevitably burn his tongue or his mouth in his eagerness and greed.

My mother still makes *zeppole* today in a small black frying pan that she inherited from her mother. She uses this priceless, battle-scarred relic solely for *zeppole* and another favourite finger food, *pitti fritti*. Though not part of the Christmas Eve feast, the latter are worth mentioning here.

Pitti fritti are palm-size fritters made from leftover pizza dough.

They are fried in olive oil like *zeppole*, left to cool for a moment, dipped in sugar, and eaten by everyone and anyone who is nearby, especially children. When making pizza, I often reserve some of the dough and keep it in the fridge overnight so I can make them for breakfast. As I said, they can be served with sugar, but they're also a perfect partner to a fried egg.*

But let's return to the *zeppole*. Another way of making them is to place a couple of anchovies in the dough as you are shaping it. I remember the first time I tried these as a very young boy and was completely repelled by the potency of the anchovies. But once I was in my teens and my palate had become more accepting of stronger flavours, I would patiently wait for those *zeppole* that my mother or grandmother had filled with anchovies. But, honestly, both versions are incredibly moreish.

Last summer I suddenly had a craving for *zeppole*, so I tried making them a couple of times, but they were not turning out properly. They weren't puffing up enough, or at all, and basically were just sort of leaden. After a second failed attempt, I was loath to throw away the dough that I had worked so hard to make, so I decided to shape it into a small round pizza of sorts and bake it in the outdoor oven. To my amazement, it puffed up beautifully and, even though I prefer my pizza thin, was absolutely delicious. The potato gave it an added depth and a billowy softness. (I love potato bread but this was quite different.) I

---

* Fry the egg in extra virgin olive oil so that the edges of the egg are crispy but the yolk is still soft, place on top of the *pitti fritti*, and add salt and pepper to taste.

then started experimenting with different toppings – sautéd peppers and goat's cheese, sautéd onions – all of which perfectly complemented the dough. With any of these toppings, a green salad and a good beer, were it offered to me as lunch or dinner, I wouldn't turn it down.

The next Christmas Eve dish that was and remains one of my favorites is *baccalà*. *Baccalà* is dried, salted cod that has been preserved by, well . . . drying and salting it, a process that has been used for millennia. Though cod comes from cold northern seas, it has found its way into the cuisine of cultures all over the world. The reason for this is that this method of preservation made it possible for it to be transported in large quantities over great distances, allowing it to be sold and traded. At one time cod was so plentiful, it was said that off the coast of Nova Scotia, people could walk across the water on the backs of this coveted fish. Unfortunately, due to overfishing, its numbers have dwindled, to say the least, hence the rather high price it commands at fishmongers' the world over.

Leading up to Christmas Eve, as had been done for centuries, my mother would reconstitute the cod by soaking it in water for a day or so. It was then rinsed to remove the excess saltiness and slowly cooked in a very light tomato sauce with potatoes and green olives. Drizzled with extra virgin olive oil and served with a piece of toasted bread, or *'fiscotto'*,* like most simple peasant dishes, it is probably one of the healthiest things one can ingest.

---

* *'Fiscotto'*, or *'biscotto'*, means 'twice cooked' in Italian. The first spelling is the Calabrese pronunciation. It is stale bread that is slowly baked at a very low temperature for a few hours. The result is a hard, toast-like bread that will keep

After the cod and other first-course dishes (there were so many I once suggested my parents build a vomitorium) came the main course. This was often a broiled bluefish.

Bluefish is not commonly eaten as most people find it oily and 'fishy'. (It is not as oily as mackerel and its meat is lighter and flakier, but it's in the same family.) However, if it's cooked properly, both of those qualities are tempered. It is also rather bony, which always put me off as a kid, but the taste was so hard to resist that I would steadily pick my way through my portion, much to my parents' dismay, with my bony little hands.

The preparation for this dish is very simple. The fish is cut in half lengthwise and sprinkled liberally with a mixture of breadcrumbs, olive oil, a little chopped garlic, chopped parsley and salt, on top of which a few thinly sliced lemon rounds are laid. It is then placed on a baking tray, loosely covered in foil, and put in the oven to bake at 160°C. After about twenty minutes to half an hour, the foil is removed and the oven is switched to broil (*grill* if you are British, still confusing for me to this day), and the fish is cooked for about five minutes to crisp and brown the top, and then left to rest for a few minutes.

Now, as you know, whenever you cook fish, your kitchen will smell like . . . well, fish. And when you cook bluefish, it will smell even *more* like fish. Not like a fish that has gone off, but just . . . *more.*

---

for a long period of time in a tin. The slow baking releases the sugars and gives it a gentle sweetness. It can be eaten with any kind of cheese or roasted peppers, or broken up into smaller pieces and dropped into soups or . . . whatever.

But don't let this stop you trying it! I promise that the delicate breadcrumb mixture and the acidity of the lemon work perfectly to nullify this particular *poisson*'s pungency, giving it an almost sweet flavour.

Over the years my parents and I would take turns hosting Christmas Eve and Christmas Day. If I were hosting Christmas Eve, I would make some of the appetizers mentioned above, but because I didn't have the time or frankly the inclination to devote myself to equalling my mother's staggering output, I would just make a huge pot of fish stew with at least seven types of seafood. I would serve it with toasted bread or sometimes use it as a sauce with pasta, usually spaghetti or linguine. It is still one of my favourite dishes to make whenever I have guests. The beauty of it is that you can use almost any type of seafood with the exception of a very oily fish, like mackerel, sardines or salmon. It takes no time at all to cook, and unless someone is allergic to shellfish, it's always a hit.

In England serving fish on Christmas Eve is not a tradition, but I still try to make at least two or three fish dishes when that night rolls around. I find them necessary light precursors to the very meat-heavy Christmas and Boxing Day meals that are soon to come.

The Christmases that I have shared with my in-laws here in England are like so many I have experienced all my life. The day is filled with gift giving, wine pouring, game playing, and, new to me, Christmas-cracker pulling. It is, however, the food that differs most from my family's Christmas Day fare, but luckily it is equally delicious, my mother-in-law Joanna being an excellent cook. There are hors d'oeuvres like 'devils on horseback' (dates wrapped in bacon and broiled to a light crisp) and tiny sausages, both of which disappear down our throats within minutes on little rivers of champagne. Unlike in an Italian meal, there is no first course (please see next chapter regarding this), but the food is bountiful: British-style roasted potatoes, steamed vegetables, and a bowl of mush called bread sauce. (Bread sauce is very white bread soaked in milk, which looks and tastes like something Mr Bumble and his ilk would have given to workhouse boys or toothless Victorian pensioners. I love everything else but it's just . . . not my favourite.)

All of these accompany a main course, which is always a grand piece of meat. Years ago it would have often been a turkey, but since my arrival into the family and the introduction of an American Thanksgiving into the calendar, we have all decided that two turkeys in a month is a bit redundant on the palate. Therefore the roast beast taking centre stage is either a three-bird roast (in America it's called a turducken, or a gooducken), which consists of either a deboned chicken stuffed inside a deboned duck, stuffed inside a deboned turkey or goose, respectively; a baked ham; a standing rib of beef; or a big fat goose all on its own. I love them all, as does everyone at the table, hence very little is left at the end of the meal. New and very welcome to my taste buds on my first British Yuletide was the classic English Christmas Day dessert sticky toffee pudding. I'm not one for sweets, but for some reason I find this very hard to resist, especially with a glass of good port that my father-in-law generously serves at the end of the meal.

After this feast we are all well sated, and as I listen to the British accents of my family, I wonder what Christmas would have been like here in days of old. I imagine donning my frock coat and top hat, wrapping my long woollen scarf around my neck, bidding farewell to my in-laws, and strolling home with my family through snowy streets lined with Georgian homes, the smoke of the coal fires within wafting from their chimneys as we make our way to the Cratchit house to check just once more on dear sweet Tiny Tim.

However, my Hollywood version of Jolly Old England is decimated when I open the front door of my in-laws' home and see it is not snowing but raining again, or *still*. The children are crying because they are leaving their grandparents, apparently forever in their minds, and we make our way into the driveway, wrestle them into their car seats as the older kids somehow squeeze into any empty space available, and cautiously drive the one mile back home before two-year-old Emilia's chronic carsickness causes her to vomit all over herself. Talk about Dickensian.

Christmas Day

Christmas mornings with three small children – as anyone will know who has three small children – are at once heartwarming and exhausting. Upon far too early an awakening, Kate and I would have to stop the kids from going after their gifts like velociraptors attacking their prey. I always kept large plastic bags at the ready and would fill them with the shredded wrapping paper as soon as it was rent from the presents by their desperate little hands. (This is to ensure that tidiness is maintained and that no present gets lost or discarded accidentally under what will soon be mounds of paper. I once threw away a beautiful antique pencil drawing I had bought for Kate as a gift, and since then I diligently employ the 'unwrap – grab the wrap – bag the wrap' method. Not a single piece of artwork or tin toy soldier has been lost since.)

After all the hubbub and the thrill of gift giving had ended and some adult relative who had come to stay was assembling a toy that I refused to assemble because I can't bear to read instructions, it was always our intention to loll around for a while in our pyjamas, sip coffee, and watch the children short-circuit as they bounced from one toy to another. Every year we imagined that these rare moments of repose were a possibility, as guests would not arrive for Christmas dinner until mid-afternoon. But every year this never happened. Here is the reason why.

———

There is a dish, a very special dish, that is served in our home on Christmas Day. It is called *timpano*. This is a baked drum of pastrylike dough filled with pasta, *ragù*, salami, various cheeses, hard-boiled eggs and meatballs. It's a big, heavy dish, and needless to say very filling. The recipe and the tradition of serving it on special occasions, particularly Christmas, were brought to America by my father's family. I never remember *not* having it on Christmas Day, whether we were celebrating at our home or at the home of one of my dad's siblings. It is quite a showstopper, so much so that we chose to feature it in *Big Night* as the centrepiece of the film's climactic meal. However, its preparation is very labour-intensive, and the cooking process requires much time and attention. It is for this last reason that, even though we would not be sitting down to eat until about two or three p.m., my parents would arrive at about eleven a.m. to begin the process of finishing the cooking of the *timpano*, which they had painstakingly assembled a couple of days before.

Upon hearing the sound of car tyres on the gravel drive and a moment later the shouts of 'Merry Christmas!' from my parents' mouths, I would sheepishly look at Kate. She would sigh quietly and then, as she slowly turned and stared at me, I would see something die in her eyes. At this point my anxiety level would skyrocket and I'd flit off to the bar to see if I couldn't find liquid calm in a bloody Mary or a Scotch sour. Laden with gifts and platters of food,* including the pièce de résistance shrouded in a large dishcloth, my elegantly dressed parents would climb the stairs smiling from ear to ear, as thrilled to see us as if we'd all been separated for decades, when in fact we had only just seen them the night before. They were so happy and excited, how could I even *think* of being put out by their extremely early arrival? (Well, perhaps not so much me as my poor wife.) I will tell you how. The *timpano*.

---

* Even though we were cooking the dinner, my mother refused not to bring at least three extra side dishes as well as any leftovers from the Christmas Eve dinner, from which we were all still recovering, because in her words, 'I'm not going to eat them and God knows your father doesn't need them!'

First let me give you the recipe so that you might acquaint your-
selves with this traditional Tucci family fare.

Timpano

— SERVES 12 TO 16 —

(THE PROPORTIONS MAY BE ADAPTED TO FIT
A SMALLER OR LARGER CONTAINER)

The dough for *timpano* is rolled out into a thin round, the diameter
of which is determined by the pan you are baking it in. Add together
the diameter of the bottom of the pan, the diameter of the top of the
pan, and twice the height of the pan. The total will equal the approxi-
mate diameter needed. The dough may be kneaded in advance and
set aside while you prepare the pan or refrigerated overnight. Return
it to room temperature before rolling it out. It is important to generously grease the pan with butter and olive oil before lining the pan
with the dough. Greasing and lining the pan with the dough may be
done while the pasta is cooking.

The meat used in preparing the *ragù* is generally served for dinner the
night before the *timpano* is baked, because no one has room for anything other than salad after eating *timpano*.

– FOR THE DOUGH –

500g plain flour, plus more for dusting

4 large eggs

1 teaspoon sea salt

3 tablespoons olive oil

125ml water

– TO PREPARE THE PAN –

Butter

Olive oil

– FOR THE FILLING –

1.3kg ziti, cooked very al dente (about half the time recommended on the package) and drained

2 tablespoons olive oil

Twice recipe quantity of Ragù Tucci (page 74), at room temperature

800g Genoa salami (5 x 10mm pieces), at room temperature

800g sharp provolone cheese (5 x 10mm cubes), at room temperature

12 hard-boiled large eggs, shelled, quartered lengthwise, and each quarter cut in half to create chunks, at room temperature

24 little meatballs, at room temperature

100g finely grated Pecorino Romano

6 large eggs, beaten

- **Make the dough:** Place the flour, eggs, salt and olive oil in the bowl of a stand mixer fitted with the dough hook. (A large-capacity food processor may also be used.) Add 3 tablespoons of the water and mix. Add more water, 1 tablespoon at a time, until the mixture comes together and forms a ball. Turn the dough out on to a lightly floured work surface and knead to make sure it is well mixed, about 10 minutes. Set aside to rest for 5 minutes.

- (To knead the dough by hand, mix the flour and salt together on a clean, dry work surface or pastry board. Form the dry ingredients into a mound and then make a well in the centre. Break the eggs into the centre of the well and beat them lightly with a fork. Stir in 3 tablespoons of the water. Use the fork to gradually incorporate some of the dry ingredients into the egg mixture. Continue mixing the dry ingredients into the eggs, adding the remaining water 1 tablespoon at a time. Knead the dough with your hands to make a well-mixed, smooth, dry dough. If the dough becomes too sticky, add more flour. Set aside to rest for 5 minutes.)

- Flatten the dough out on a lightly floured work surface. Dust the top of the dough with flour and roll it out, dusting with flour and flipping the dough over from time to time to keep it from sticking to the board, until it is about 2mm thick and the desired diameter.

- **Prepare the pan:** Grease the *timpano* baking pan very generously with butter and olive oil so that it is well lubricated. Fold the dough in half and then in half again to form a triangle and place it in the pan. Unfold the dough and arrange it in the pan, gently pressing it against the bottom and the side and draping the extra dough over the side. Set aside.

- Preheat the oven to 180°C.

- **Make the filling:** Toss the drained pasta with the olive oil and allow it to cool slightly before tossing with a quarter of the *ragù*. Distribute about a quarter of the pasta over the dough on the bottom of the *timpano*. Top with a quarter of the salami, a quarter of the provolone, 3 of the hard-boiled eggs, a quarter of the meatballs, and a third of the Romano cheese. Pour another quarter of the *ragù* over these ingredients. Repeat this process to create additional layers using an equal amount of each ingredient until they have come within 2cm of the top of the pan, ending with a final layer of the *ragù*. Pour the beaten eggs over the filling. Fold the dough over the filling to seal completely. Trim away and discard any overlapping dough. Make sure that the *timpano* is tightly sealed. If you notice any small openings, cut a piece of the trimmed dough to fit over the opening, using a small amount of water to moisten the scraps to ensure a tight seal has been made.

- Bake until lightly browned, about 1 hour. Then cover with aluminium foil and continue baking until the dough is golden-brown and the *timpano* is cooked through (and reaches an internal temperature of 48°C), about 30 minutes. Remove from the oven and allow to rest for 30 minutes to cool and contract before attempting to remove from the pan. (The baked *timpano* should not adhere to the pan. To test, gently shake the pan to the left and then to the right. It should spin slightly in the pan. If any part is still attached, carefully detach with a knife.)

- To remove the *timpano* from the pan, place a baking sheet or thin cutting board that's large enough to cover the entire diameter of the pan on top of the *timpano*. Grasp the baking sheet or cutting board and the rim of the *timpano* pan firmly and invert the *timpano*. Remove the pan and allow the *timpano* to cool for 30 minutes more.

- Using a long, sharp knife, cut a circle approximately 8cm in diameter in the centre of the *timpano*, making sure to cut all the way through to the bottom. Then slice the *timpano* into individual portions as you would a pie, leaving the centre circle as a support for the remaining pieces. The cut pieces should hold together, revealing the built-up layers of great stuff.

It is the inconstant cooking and resting times required of each individual *timpano* made any given year that became the bane of Christmas Day. It is a temperamental dish to say the least. It might take an hour or two to cook, then need to rest for an hour, or vice versa. It depends on the oven, the vessel it's cooked in, if the sauce it is made with is a little more watery than usual, if the *timpano* has been previously frozen, etc., etc. That's all fine, *if* it is the only thing you are serving. But *timpano* was served as a *first course*. Therefore it was impossible to time the second course, like a leg of lamb or even a simple ham. People often wonder why, if there is such a huge first course, there is even a need for a second course at all. I have no answer for them. All I know is that it is traditional. It is very rare that one eats in an Italian home and both a *primo* and a *secondo* are not served on any given day. I remember the first time my brother-in-law John came to visit us in Westchester, my parents were over and my mother had cooked. She served the Tucci family *ragù* with pasta, followed by the *ragù* meat and meatballs. Obviously finding it delicious, John kept going back for more. After a while, bowls and plates were cleared and new plates laid, at which point my mother brought a roast chicken, potatoes, two different vegetables and a salad to the table. I noticed that John was suddenly a bit rattled. Confounded by what was basically another entire meal being placed before him, he politely asked, 'Wow, wait, what's all this?'

'What do you mean?' asked my mother, equally confounded by his query. 'It's dinner.'

'*Still?!*' He gawped. 'I mean, well, what was that, that we just ate?'

'That was just the first course,' said my father, grinning devilishly.

'Oh my God! I thought –'

'You thought that was *it*, didn't you?' I asked.

'Well, yeah. I mean, I had three helpings!'

'I had a feeling you thought that was the main course!'

'Are you kidding?! You can't have just that. Especially on a Sunday!' chastised my mother.

Needless to say, we dug into the chicken and vegetables with gusto.

Two courses. It's just the way it has always been, and on holidays both courses just get bigger. A lasagna, a bowl of pasta, or a soup as a first course is perfectly acceptable, but as I say, *timpano* can cause issues both culinary and marital. How many over- or undercooked, not inexpensive pieces of meat were angrily eaten by Kate due to her inability to time them appropriately because of the *timpano*, I cannot say. Not only were those legs or hocks lovingly prepared by her but also, they were what she was looking forward to eating, because she didn't even *like timpano*. (It's sort of like cilantro; you either like it or you don't. I happen to love it.) But even if the meal miraculously ended up being timed perfectly, the *timpano* was so rich and heavy that the meat course could not be enjoyed to the fullest. At any rate, somehow we ate our way through just about everything most Christmases, but not without a lingering resentment deep in Kate's soul.

I am of course being a bit harsh when I make it seem as though Christmases were ruined completely by an inanimate drum of pasta-filled pastry, but sometimes it came close. As I said, usually a ham or leg of lamb was served. The ham would be a large bone-in shank, studded with cloves and a few pineapple rings and basted with a brown-sugar glaze. It was then left to rest and served with potatoes, either roasted or au gratin, and string beans. If we were serving lamb, it was salted and drizzled with olive oil, and incisions were made with a small knife, into which garlic and rosemary were inserted. A little white wine mixed with the meat juices made a light and savoury gravy. The sweet smell of a leg of lamb roasting in the oven still brings back so many happy holiday memories for me. Throughout most of the world lamb is eaten a great deal but it seems to have fallen out of favour in America, and I am not sure why, as it is delicious and can be cooked so many ways.*

After dinner, espresso, *digestivi*, fruit, nuts, dates, dried figs, biscotti and Lazzaroni amaretti cookies were served. These little almond-flavoured rounds came wrapped in a delicate, crinkly, opaque paper. My father's favourite party trick was to roll the paper into a tube, stand it upright on the dinner table, and light the top of it on fire. If done properly it would burn down evenly, and, while somehow maintaining its cylindrical shape, just before the flame reached the bottom and singed the tablecloth, the now-blackened paper would float high up into the air and almost, but never, touch the ceiling. What properties cause it to become aerodynamic when ignited are a mystery, but I know of no other paper in the world that has this ability. As kids we begged my dad to do it over and over again, and he was more than willing to oblige, often to my mother's dismay. The reason being that there were a few instances when there was a 'failure to launch' and certain precious tablecloths still bear the scars.

After dinner, dessert, and semi-drunken conversations about

---

* The English and the Italians love lamb, and places like Australia and New Zealand are famous for theirs, yet perhaps the most delicious lamb I have ever eaten was in Iceland. I will address this in another chapter.

politics or something vaguely serious were attempted, the furniture was cleared to the edges of the living room, and the 'Ring Game' was played. This is a game of deception in which lying and cheating are encouraged. There are no teams and there is no winner. A ring is threaded on to a long piece of string, which is then tied together at the ends. A circle is formed by the players, who hold the circle of string in both fists at waist height. One person is placed in the middle of the circle, whose goal it is to find out which player is hiding the ring. The person who has been found to have the ring then takes their place in the centre. As soon as the game commences, all players begin sliding their hands in both directions, either *pretending* to pass the ring or *actually* passing the ring to the players on either side of them, shouting wildly things like, 'Here, you take it! I don't want it!' etc. etc. Needless to say, the poor person in the middle is slowly driven mad. The better you were at slipping the ring into the fist of the person next to you, and they were caught with it by the person in the middle, the less likely *you* were to end up in the middle. It is a cruel but brilliantly funny game, and as soon as you understand that cheating is not only necessary but *fair*, as it sometimes is in life, you will enjoy it.

At the end of the day, when all the guests had gone and the children were tucked away after endlessly caterwauling about not being tired, Kate and I would end up having the 'inevitable conversation'. It is important for you to know that this was a woman with the patience of a saint, a woman who seldom complained about *anything*. But by the light of the Christmas tree, as I sipped a late-night Scotch, the words, 'That *fucking timpano* . . . ', would hiss from her lips and a discussion about tradition, how not to insult family, or whether we should just go skiing over Christmas, etc., would ensue.

However, I must admit that while the rest of the family slept, midnight often found me by the open refrigerator, eating a huge piece of *timpano* and secretly thinking that for all its trouble, it was probably the best fucking Christmas gift of all.

A Yule Epilogue

My wife Felicity Blunt and I started dating in the autumn of 2010 (thrilling details await you in an upcoming chapter), and about a year or so later she moved to Westchester to live with me and the kids. When Felicity spent her first Christmas with us, I was hoping she might take to *timpano* differently than Kate had. That didn't happen. What happened was exactly what I have described in the previous pages. I am not kidding. Exactly. Pre-dawn Christmas Day parental arrivals, roasted meats brought to the table dry or charred like pathetic afterthoughts, the rolling of eyes, the gnashing of teeth by a woman (who also has a saintlike patience) at the mere *mention* of *timpano*, and of course the inevitable late-night conversation beginning with the words, now uttered darkly in a posh British accent, 'That *fucking timpano* . . .'

A Christmas Cocktail

Here is my holiday version of a Cosmopolitan.

– SERVES 1 –

1 tablespoon pomegranate seeds
50ml Ketel One vodka
25ml Cointreau
25ml cranberry juice (either unsweetened or cranberry
juice cocktail. Your preference)
25ml pomegranate juice
Ice
1 raspberry, 1 mint leaf and fresh rosemary, to garnish

- Put the pomegranate seeds into a shaker and muddle until muddled.

- Add the booze.

- Add the juices.

- Add the ice.

- Shake it.

- Strain into a coupe or a Martini glass.

- Garnish with a raspberry wrapped in a mint leaf and skewered with a small stalk of rosemary.

- Drink it and have a happier holiday.

8

Films and television were crucial to my development as a kid and stand accused for causing me to choose the occupation I have devoted myself to for almost forty years. At around the age of ten, I would go to the movies every Saturday with a friend and see whatever was showing in a nearby movie theatre that our parents had deemed appropriate for our innocent eyes. (I remember sitting through a *Planet of the Apes* marathon one Saturday and emerging from the theatre bleary-eyed, exhausted, and, because I'd spent so long in an altered reality, very confused as to why there were no simians on the streets of Mount Kisco.) Although I did enjoy reading, especially anything to do with the Second World War, I also spent so much time watching old movies on our black and white Zenith television that my parents had to pry me away from it over and over again. On certain afternoons there was the *Million Dollar Movie* on Channel 9. This was usually some classic drama to which I would glue myself as I ate an excessive number of buttered hard rolls or peanut butter sandwiches. I was also addicted to so many of the classic television shows of the sixties and seventies, like *The Rat Patrol*, *The Brady Bunch*, *The Wild Wild West* and *Lost in Space*. (The latter three, for better or for worse, would become Hollywood films over thirty years later.) I also loved watching cooking shows, and as the years went on there were more and more of them on WNET, the New York City PBS station. Just as certain actors led me to acting, there are two television cooking show hosts who had a profound impact upon me and are partly to blame for my heightened interest in the subject of food.

Watching someone cook on camera is fascinating, and these two people did it better than anyone in my opinion. The first is of course the queen of culinary TV, Julia Child. The second would be her prince, Keith Floyd. I shall begin by addressing the queen, as she always deserves to come first.

Julia Child

Julia Child changed not only what Americans cooked and ate but greatly impacted their diet of weekly television viewing. Her show *The French Chef*, which originally aired in 1963, was one of the first cooking shows on American television and lasted for ten years. Watching her expertly debone a chicken or make a tarte Tatin, often making mistakes along the way, made viewers feel that they too could create such dishes themselves. Her achievements in the world of food are staggering, from her first and seminal work, *Mastering the Art of French Cooking*, to countless others, as well as season upon season of shows hosted either alone or with other great talents, like Jacques Pépin, about the art and craft of cooking.

Much has also been written about her, including *Julie and Julia*, a wonderful book that was made into a film of the same name in which I was fortunate enough to appear. I don't know that I have much to write on the subject of making the film that would fit these pages, but I can say it was a great honour to be asked by Meryl Streep and Nora Ephron to play the role of Paul Child.* It was one of those rare working experiences, not unlike *The Devil Wears Prada*, that one wishes could be repeated. (Obviously there's probably one reason for this, but I won't give her the credit.)

Anyway, ever since I was very young, Julia Child has always fascinated me. My mother tuned in to *The French Chef* religiously, and I remember watching with her and loving it. I don't know, however, if it was my mother's keen interest in everything that Julia did or Julia's keen interest in everything that she *herself* was doing that I found so captivating. However, I do know that watching *The French Chef* with my mom was a way to spend some time with her, because with three kids and a full-time job, she was incredibly busy. In fact, we would often watch the show when she was ironing or folding laundry, as just watching television without doing something productive simultaneously was anathema to her. I personally still struggle

---

* Actually I do have a tale to tell regarding *Julie and Julia*. See page 187.

to sit and watch a film because I always feel that there are too many tasks I need to accomplish. This strange sense of guilt makes no sense, because as an actor, writer and director, it is my *business* to watch as much as possible. Yet for the most part, I only watch something while exercising or at the end of the night, when the younger kids are in bed, dinner is complete, and the kitchen is in order. However, at this point I am usually so tired, it's a bit of a struggle to last very long.

Anyway, after that unnecessary information about my psyche, as Julia was working away on a batch of crêpes or making a soufflé, my mother would comment out loud about her process. Asides such as 'Huh, so *that's* how you do that,' or 'Well, I think that's a little *too* much butter,' or 'Isn't she just so *great*?!' were heard as she flicked water from her fingers on to a cotton shirt neatly draped over the ironing board. My mother adored and admired Julia Child and in turn imparted those feelings to me, along with an avid interest in how someone goes about cooking a meal.

To that point, I remember when visiting my parents' years later, I happened to catch an old episode of *The French Chef*. Because my interest in food had grown, I watched it with even more attentiveness than I had when I was young. But on this particular occasion, I was taken aback by my reaction when Mrs Child bid us her ubiquitous farewell, 'This is Julia Child, bon appétit!' My eyes suddenly welled up and I had to stop myself from crying. Why was I suddenly experiencing a powerful rush of emotion because a black and white moving image of a chef was saying goodbye to me in French? After a few moments, I realized that I was moved by Mrs Child not only because she brought back happy boyhood memories of spending time with my mom but also because Julia herself was so genuinely happy to be doing what she was doing. I saw in that moment the embodiment of what I, and so many of us, aspire to. To spend your life doing what you love and doing it well. To achieve this is a rare thing, but for those who can, *real* joy is theirs, as is the ability to bring that joy to others through their chosen vocation.

Although Julia Child struggled in early adulthood to find a profession that suited her intellect, curiosity and lust for life, as well as one that would make her happy, she more than made up for it over the years, from the time she made her first omelette to the time she wished us all a final breathy 'Bon appétit!' She also inspired and made millions of people the world over very happy, including a mother and son in Westchester, New York, over fifty years ago.

Keith Floyd

American audiences may not be as familiar with Keith Floyd as they are with Julia Child or many of the television food personalities on today's screens (too many, as far as I'm concerned, but who am I to talk?), but for the Brits and for me as well, Floyd set the gold standard for the television food travelogue. In episode after episode, he conquers the recipes of entire countries as he swills glasses of wine while eruditely displaying an encyclopedic knowledge of their cuisine.

If you have never seen his show, it is now easily found on

YouTube and is a real treat for any food lover. The format of the show is basic. Floyd travels to a foreign country or a region of England and cooks classic local dishes in kitchens borrowed from farmers, landed gentry, housewives, fishermen and chefs. He also often cooks '*en plein air*'. In one episode of *Floyd on Spain*, he cooks a pork stew in the Spanish countryside. In an episode of *Floyd on Italy*, he makes a local pasta dish in the piazza of a small Italian town, and in another, a fish stew aboard a fishing boat in rough waters. When filming in a public place, the handheld camera candidly catches the locals as they look on bewildered, amused, and even annoyed as this mad Brit in a bow tie and braces conjures up their traditional dishes with a booze-fuelled fervour while prattling away non-stop to the camera.

I recently watched an episode that took place in a small home kitchen that he had commandeered in Provence. The sequence begins with a continuous six-minute take, something you would never see on a cooking show today. Floyd starts out with a sip of wine as he shows us a sink full of fish he has bought at a local market for a Provençal fish stew he's about to make. He directs the camera operator to get a shot of this and a shot of that as he describes the types of fish, then directs the fellow to follow him, colander of fish in hand, as he moves over to the stove, explains the base for the stew, dumps the fish in a pot, adds some hot water, then swiftly moves over to the oven, takes out a chicken that is roasting, explains the manner in which he has prepared it but tells us how the matron of the house told him he had done it improperly, and then says he doesn't really care what she thinks and he doesn't *really* know *everything* about French cooking anyway as he deftly makes his way back to the stove where in four separate pans simmer the ingredients of a ratatouille, explains each one individually, then combines them and wraps up the sequence with a sip of wine and a comment about needing a break. He does all this for six minutes straight without a pause. If you have ever tried to film yourself, or have someone film you, preparing even the simplest recipe while talking to camera, you will know that it is close to impossible to do it without having to cut and reset countless times. It is most likely that you will make mistakes again and again and will eventually have to edit the bits and pieces together later on. To sustain a take for six minutes and keep it interesting and entertaining is a feat I challenge any of today's television chefs to attempt. Is the production quality of Floyd's show the greatest? Hardly. But his energy, excitement, and profound knowledge about what he's doing, along with some impressive handheld camerawork, make for an incredibly dynamic and entertaining cooking show.

In one episode he is hunkered down with the Royal Navy somewhere in Cornwall and cooks Portuguese man-of-war (a dish I had never heard of that combines pork, onions, tomato, and a variety of molluscs) in rectangular pans over a makeshift stove of mud and bricks on a characteristically miserable grey English afternoon, while slurping rum from a teacup. The whole sequence, which is composed of only a few shots, happens very quickly and is as wonderfully entertaining as it is bizarre. Do we know how the dish tastes? No, we don't. But does it really matter? Not to me.

Floyd made us feel like any one of us could make any of the

dishes he made even with the most rudimentary kitchen kit, the most primitive fire source, in the worst weather, in the middle of fucking nowhere, while swilling just about anything alcoholic from a tin can. Besides being entertaining, whether he was roughing it or cooking in the kitchen of a Michelin-starred restaurant, Floyd was incredibly informative, and you walked away from each show feeling that you had actually learned something about the history and culture that were the root of the dishes he prepared with such assurance. He did this without being precious or pedantic, spitting out the information quickly as he chopped, stirred, sautéd, basted, and of course, in his words, 'slurped'.

He died at the age of sixty-five of a heart attack. Too many years of smoking and excessive drinking took their toll on an autodidactic cook who taught real chefs more than a thing or two and gave great pleasure to many food lovers all over the globe. What Keith Floyd did by taking the cooking show out of the studio into the streets, on to the seas and up to the mountaintops changed the face of food television for better and forever. Those of us in that world should take a lesson from his irreverent improvisatory style and follow in his peripatetic footsteps.

———

I remember my acting teacher George Morrison telling us that audiences love to watch people eating, drinking or smoking on stage and screen. This always stuck with me. As usual, he was more than right. Having seen countless films and plays since my college days, I know there is indeed something very compelling about watching someone carry out a very necessary mundane task. It humanizes them and therefore allows us to connect to them. It's probably one of the reasons why people love food movies and there are so many cooking shows on television now. Also, we want to see the process, either because it's something we love to do ourselves or because it's something we aspire to do. But we also want to see the reaction to the *result* of the process because we aren't there to taste it ourselves. Was all that effort worth it? Could I do that? Does it taste as good as it looks? Or, perhaps most important, does it really taste as good as they're saying it does?

This is a bit of a bugbear of mine. Whether it is an actor, a chef or a cook, I think you can always tell when someone isn't *really* tasting something. You don't even have to look that closely to see that this happens too often on the excessive number of cooking shows that inundate today's television. It seems that before whatever is being eaten has touched the tongue of the chef/host/cook, they are rolling their eyes in ecstasy, moaning and shaking their heads as if it's the most delicious thing ever to have crossed their lips. To make matters worse, before they have even finished swallowing, the word 'perfect' is sanctimoniously whispered.

All I can say is, no. No. Sorry. I don't believe you. There is no possible way that you are *actually tasting* whatever you ate that quickly and that whatever the hell you made is actually that extraordinary. And who the fuck ever, even brilliant chefs, makes something that is 'perfect' right out of the gate every time? More often than not, there is something not quite right. It's too sweet, or not sweet enough, or needs more salt or pepper or oil, or there's too much . . . whatever! To see someone adjust seasoning or comment on what has worked or doesn't work in a dish is a thousand times more interesting and instructive than their giving themselves a clearly false pat on the back for their culinary genius.

When someone *really* tastes something, whatever process happens in their mouth triggers a reaction in their eyes as well as the rest of their body. First, the body almost freezes, as though it were on high alert, and then people will often tilt their heads to one side, usually to the left, and look like they are listening very carefully to something as they are chewing. Often their heads will nod slowly, their eyes darting back and forth. At times their eyes will lock, staring straight ahead for a moment, and then they'll glance down to the left and then to the right. After all of this, which can happen in an instant or take quite some time, they will utter a sound of approval or disappointment, such as, 'Mmmm', if they like it, or 'Mnnnn', if they don't. They will then say something like, 'Good. I like it,' or, 'I should have ordered the steak.'

Watch Julia Child taste something and you'll see what I mean.

———————

Inspired by these two multitalented pioneers, I recently embarked on a project in which I tried to put their teachings to good use, *Searching for Italy*. If you haven't seen it, I of course take umbrage but will rise above your insult, ignore your ignorance and give you a quick synopsis. The show is a documentary series filmed on and off during 2019 and 2020. Each episode focuses on the food of one Italian region and the forces that helped shape it, in order to show the extraordinary diversity of the country's cuisine. Because of where Italy sits geographically, it has been invaded and controlled by countless cultures over the past two thousand years. Those cultures have influenced the cuisine as significantly as the widely varied topography of the peninsula, which stretches from the Alps to the southern Mediterranean. (For instance, Punta Pesce Spada, which means 'Swordfish Point', on the island of Lampedusa, is only ninety-six miles from the coast of North Africa. In Val d'Aosta, one of Italy's regions on the Swiss border, is its most northern point, Westliches Zwillingsköpfl, which in German means 'Jesus Christ, is it cold here, or is it just me?!' It doesn't actually mean that, but you take my point.)

During the shoot I encountered some extraordinarily talented people, from chefs, to home cooks, to farmers and purveyors, not to mention an endless supply of delicious dishes. I would like to include them all here, but this book would end up as a six-volume set. Besides, I don't have the time to write it because I have to go out and make a living, so you'll just have to tune in to the show. (Please check your local listings for viewing times.) However, I have chosen three different dishes, one from the north, one from the middle of the country, and one from the far south. I have done so because I believe they represent the wonderful diversity of the Italian table. Their only commonality is that they are all made with some type of pasta.

Pizzoccheri

Le Alpi

One of the most beautiful regions of Italy, in my opinion, is Lombardy, situated in the very north of the country and home to Milan, Lake Como and the Orobic Alps. Like other northern regions, its food varies primarily from that of the south due to topography and climate. In these mountains where the land sees quite a bit of rain and snow, tomatoes and eggplant are not as prevalent as root vegetables and cabbage. Grain grown for pasta throughout the southern parts of Italy gives way to corn (both yellow and white, used to make polenta), rice (for risotto) and buckwheat. It is with the latter that one of my favourite dishes ever is made, the traditional Lombard recipe known as pizzoccheri.

Pizzoccheri is a noodle composed of approximately 50 per cent buckwheat flour and 50 per cent wheat flour, about the length and width of pappardelle but a bit thicker and more dense. It is served during the autumn and winter months in a kind of casserole called *pappardelle alla Valtellina*. Valtellina. The name sounds like that of an imagined zaftig wood sprite from a Fellini film. Good God, what a gorgeous chunk of Alpine cheese is Valtellina. Its soft and gentle creaminess when melted just wraps itself around –

Off to take a cold shower.

I'm back.

Anyway, pizzoccheri, like most Italian food, comes from humble beginnings and has a rightful place in the canon of Cucina

Povera. Using very few ingredients, it creates an extremely rich and hearty dish. After a winter's day outdoors in the Alps, like raclette or venison stew it is exactly what a body wants and needs. But there is one more key ingredient that elevates this dish, another cheese, called Bitto.

In the tiniest of tiny Italian mountain towns, Gerola Alta, Paolo Ciapparelli is carrying on the age-old tradition of making this historic cheese. Bitto is made from the milk of cows that graze on the Alpine mountain flora. Since the pastures are at different altitudes and receive differing amounts of sun and moisture, the flora vary, and they each impart their particular flavours to the cow's milk. Bitto has been made this way for centuries, yet new EU regulations, which are often at odds with traditional methods, have allowed the cheese-making process to omit crucial steps and add new ones, therefore altering its true character and taste. For this reason, with the support of the Slow Food movement, Paolo has chosen to continue making Bitto the old way, calling it Bitto Storico (Historic Bitto) or Bitto Ribelle (Rebel Bitto).

Historic Bitto is made with the addition of about 10 per cent indigenous Orobic goat's milk. The addition of goat's milk allows the cheese to be aged for an extraordinary amount of time, usually for about five to twelve years but sometimes up to eighteen years. This is unheard of in the world of cheese making. The depth of flavour this amount of ageing imparts is the reason it is the most expensive cheese in the world, selling for over six thousand dollars for a twenty-kilo wheel.

Visiting Paolo's *casera* (cheese cellar) is basically like entering a museum of aroma. The rich, deep, complex smells coming from a thousand wheels of cheese caused even my nostrils and my eyes to salivate. It was almost overwhelming. As I was about to rip open a wheel with my bare hands and gnaw my way through it, I noticed that Paolo had laid out three cheeses of various ages for me to taste, along with some local wines, hence saving me from an embarrassingly feral public episode. The differences between them were distinct, the oldest cheese being the most dry and most potent, the youngest slightly softer, and the cheese aged for a certain amount of time between the two tasted unsurprisingly like a bit of both. This is the same experience one might have when tasting Parmigiano in varying states of age. However, each morsel of the triad of Bitto had an extraordinary complexity and depth of flavour that I had never tasted in a cheese before. I cannot explain it other than to say it was exactly the sum of its parts and then some: mountains, rain, snow, cows, goats, grass and time. Although I know that Parmigiano is known as the 'King of Cheeses', on a blustery day in a cellar in Gerola Alta in the Orobic Alps, according to this palate, that milky throne was usurped by tiny fragments of three ancient wheels of Bitto.

After visiting Paolo that day in his subterranean lactic lair, I went to a small stone cottage farther up in the mountains where I had promised to make pizzoccheri for the crew using a hunk of Bitto gifted by Paolo. As we made our way up to the cottage, I began to panic. What the *fuck* was I *thinking*? I had only made the dish a couple of times before and it had never quite turned out the way I had hoped. (I had eaten it for the first time at Riva, a London restaurant run by Andrea Riva, who hails from Lombardy, where it is made to perfection, hence my obsession.) As my panic was peaking we arrived at this gorgeous but tiny stone cottage that had been in the same family for generations. Once a barn for animals, it had been renovated into a charming weekend retreat. We were greeted by the owners, three generations of them: the grandfather, in his eighties, his daughter, and her teenage children. Suddenly I realized I was not only making pizzoccheri for the crew (who had no idea what it was supposed to taste like and were always starving, so I could easily get away with a mediocre version), but I was to prepare it for the family as well, all of whom were Lombards and knew this dish better than anyone in the world. Especially the octogenarian patriarch!

I took a deep breath, poured an enormous glass of cold white wine, and basically 'acted'. Yes, dear reader, as you have seen me do for close to forty years now on stages and screens big and small, I simply *pretended* that I had been making pizzoccheri since birth. I moved with swift assurance as I talked through the steps while the cameras rolled, and within about forty minutes, from the initial pasta-making process to the final grate of Bitto, I served up the best pizzoccheri I have ever made and probably will ever make. Even the grandfather devoured his and told me it was perfect.

He was to die that night.

Kidding.

How did I do it?

Why did it work?

When fear grips the soul, it's amazing what one can achieve. Especially when the cameras are rolling.

Now, I am sure that the indigenous ingredients, local buckwheat flour, sweet white Alpine butter, voluptuous Valtellina cheese, and of course the Bitto had a great deal to do with the successful outcome. I would also not be afraid to suggest that the comforting ambience of a stone cottage heated by an old woodstove as a mix of rain and snow blanketed the foothills of the Italian Alps perhaps played a significant role as well. As they say, location, location, Bitto, acting.

Here is how pizzoccheri is made and what you must do in order to truly understand why the dish was created ages ago.

First, make sure it's cold out. Then, go for a hike up a mountain or partake in some winter activity such as skiing, skating, wood chopping, Alpine cow milking, hunting, ice fishing, axe throwing, or perhaps . . . cheese making.

Pizzoccheri

=======

– SERVES 4 TO 6 –

1 medium Savoy cabbage
A big sexy slab of Valtellina cheese, or something similar, like fontina
2 handfuls of grated Parmigiano-Reggiano, or Bitto
(if available and you can afford it)
3 large yellow potatoes
A fuck of a lot of butter
4 large garlic cloves
500g pizzoccheri
Extra virgin olive oil
Salt

- Remove and discard any tough outer leaves from the cabbage and roughly chop it into long pieces. Thinly cut about 15 pieces of Valtellina cheese and also grate about 200g. Grate the Parmigiano. Set aside.

- Preheat the oven to 160°C.

- Peel and dice the potatoes and boil until cooked but still firm, about 15 minutes or so. Halfway through boiling, add the cabbage to the potatoes. When the potatoes and cabbage are cooked, drain them and set them aside.

- In a large, deep frying pan over low heat, melt the fuckload of butter. Gently crush (if that's even possible) the garlic cloves, place them in the pan, and cook until they soften and the butter has melted but not turned brown.

- Boil the pizzoccheri until al dente and drain, reserving about two cupfuls of the water. Return the pizzoccheri to the pot and drizzle them with a little olive oil or some butter so they don't stick together. Pour a little of the garlic butter into a baking dish and begin to layer the ingredients, starting with the pizzoccheri, then the cabbage, then the potatoes, then both cheeses, drizzling more garlic butter over the whole mixture after each layer, adding a bit of the reserved pasta water to ensure it doesn't get too thick but making sure it doesn't get too watery. You may need only a cupful. Top the final layer with a drizzle of olive oil and more grated cheese.

- Cover with foil and bake for about 15 minutes or so. Remove the foil and return to the oven until the top has a slight crisp. Salt to taste.

- Serve it and eat it and drink a lot of wine with it and think about how much you deserve it after you burned off so many calories being so active in the frigid out-of-doors.

Carbonara

Roma

Spaghetti alla carbonara.

Fuck.

It's incredible.

Especially at this one place in Rome.

FUCK!!!!

Allow me to better articulate.

Unlike pizzoccheri, carbonara is universally known and loved by pasta devotees, but there are so many iterations of it that I am compelled to set the record as straight as a record can be set straight in the complex and personal world of Italian cooking regarding what makes a *true* carbonara.

No one really knows the genesis of this rich and unctuous dish, but supposedly the basis of this typical Roman fare was invented by shepherds in the hills of Lazio who brought pasta, *guanciale* and Parmigiano or Pecorino Romano with them when they went to tend their flocks. The combination of those ingredients would become known as pasta '*alla Gricia*' and it is the addition of eggs that creates '*alla carbonara*'. It has also been posited that carbonara was actually a post-World War II invention of the Romans to satisfy the palates of the American and British soldiers who pined for their breakfasts of ham and eggs. I must admit this rings dubiously to these ears, as well as to those of Aldo, the owner of the Roman restaurant Pommidoro, which serves what is to many, including me, the best carbonara in a city of carbonaras.

Aldo was eight years of age when his family home and restaurant in Rome was bombed by the Americans in an attempt to flush out the German troops as the Allies worked their way northward into the city. With the exception of him and his father, his entire family was killed in the blast. Fortunately after the war the neighbours helped them rebuild both their home and the restaurant. Aldo is now in his eighties, and he and his restaurant are still very active and consistently turning out what is probably indeed the best *spaghetti alla carbonara* that I've ever tasted. Hence my profane outburst above.

As with most recipes, it is the quality of the ingredients that makes this dish greater than the sum of its parts. *Guanciale* (cured pork cheek) from local breeders, eggs from naturally raised chickens, traditionally made and aged Pecorino or Parmigiano, and high-quality dried pasta (Aldo recommends Cav. Giuseppe Cocco spaghetti, which can be easily found online) are the only ingredients necessary to create a meal that somehow manages to be as elegant as it is rustic. I have a recipe for carbonara in the cookbook that Felicity and I wrote together years ago, *The Tucci Table*, and even though it is tasty, like many recipes, it is something of a bastardization of the dish. In a *true* carbonara, *only guanciale* is used and *never* pancetta. There is no onion or garlic and certainly *never, ever* any cream or butter. People often think that the latter two ingredients are necessary in order to give the dish its proper creaminess when in fact this effect is achieved by not only the combination of egg yolks, cheese and pasta water but the timing of when they are incorporated.

Aldo's daughter made this classic dish so effortlessly for me the day we filmed. To watch her do so was revelatory. Gorgeous fatty, peppery strips of *guanciale* are sautéd in a deep saucepan. Once they have rendered, al dente spaghetti is placed in the pan with them. The heat is turned off as a mixture of whole eggs and egg yolks is poured in. Everything is then gently tossed together with handfuls of Parmigiano and some of the starchy pasta water.

When I tasted it I could not help but hug Aldo. The flavour had such depth that it practically penetrated my soul. It was like I'd met a wonderfully kind long-lost sibling I never knew existed and with whom I could now spend time for the rest of my life.

Okay, maybe my reactions are a bit extreme.

But I dare you to go to Pommidoro, eat the carbonara, and not just shout something like:

'FUCK!'

One can even make carbonara within a hollowed-out wheel of Parmigiano. After combining the *guanciale*, egg and pasta, place the mixture in the hollowed-out wheel and toss gently with a large fork and spoon, scraping the cheese from the bottom and sides of the wheel as you do so. The hot pasta will melt the cheese, making this action very easy, and create a silken viscosity that makes for a great bit of culinary theatre, besides being a cheese lover's wet dream.

Spaghetti alla Bottarga

Sicilia

Whenever I am travelling for work, especially to places with which I don't feel an affinity, finding *any* affinity with *anything* is crucial. It will not surprise you to know that I attempt to find an affinity with the food. I usually seek out small restaurants that are well practised in preparing classic dishes. Obviously I am always drawn to an Italian menu, but I may find a French, Japanese or Chinese place that serves up well-prepared old standards. After long days of filming in odd locations and too many weeks alone in hotels, a good restaurant with consistently well-cooked classic fare is as close to home as one can get. One of my go-to comfort dishes is a rather odd one, and not often easily found: *spaghetti alla bottarga*.

Bottarga is dried fish roe, usually from red mullet or bluefin tuna. It's used in abundance in southern Italy and Sardinia, where those fish are plentiful, and grated on to pasta or sometimes sliced thinly and served on bread. It is pungent and salty with just the right amount of fishiness to lift a bowl of spaghetti to new places, not unlike truffles do to anything they encounter. Like all things salty, *bottarga* is quite addictive. Whenever I have splurged (it's not cheap) and procured a chunk, I find myself not only making *pasta alla bottarga* but grating it on any- and everything. I've rained it upon eggs, shrimp risotto and *spaghetti alle vongole*, and all are delicious. (In Sardinian restaurants its presence is practically inescapable.) If there's a precious block of it in front of me I struggle to stop myself from slicing it paper-thin, popping that wafer of concentrated roe in my mouth, and just letting it melt. Of course you can only eat so many of these briny biscuits before you become completely dehydrated. Whenever I end up in Los Angeles (always against my will), I often head directly from the airport to Madeo,* a wonderful Italian restaurant on Beverly Boulevard, and order *spaghetti alla bottarga* because they make it so well. I don't know why I find it so comforting. Yes, the salt is appealing, but maybe it's the utter simplicity of the dish that attracts me.

When we filmed our episode about Sicily, we had the good fortune to interview a self-taught chef named Tony Lo Coco. Tony, who has the solid build of a rugby player and a handsome bald head that deserves to be sculpted one day, lives with his family on the outskirts of Palermo in the town of Bagheria. It is there, in his tiny, elegant Michelin-starred restaurant, I Pupi, that he has been transforming classic Sicilian dishes into modern marvels for quite some time now, and one of his specialties is *spaghetti alla bottarga*.

Tony and his wife are warm, open-hearted people with whom I felt instantly at home. Although he spoke no English and had to suffer through my Italian, we hit it off instantly. On the day of filming we started rolling our cameras in the kitchen, where Tony showed me how he makes *his* version of my favourite saline bowl of carbs. (Afterwards I also ate a number of his other dishes, including a flight of

---

* While revising this chapter, I discovered that Madeo has closed. I don't know the reason why, but like so many customers, I am heartbroken.

Sicilian sashimi. Seven varieties of fish, each paired with a different homemade flavoured oil and salt. My fingers can't find the words to describe it.)

To begin, this creative and physical powerhouse of a man makes his own pasta dough. He then puts it through a machine with a perforated bronze plate at the end, and the dough emerges in strands of thick spaghetti. The bronze gives the pasta a rough surface, allowing the sauce to cling to it more easily. (I'm buying one tomorrow.) A little olive oil and a little garum are drizzled into a hot pan. Garum is a fermented fish sauce that has been made for millennia in varying forms by many cultures to impart umami flavour to a variety of dishes. The version Tony uses is made with anchovies and is known as *colatura di alici*. The cooked spaghetti is then placed in the pan and tossed with the oil, the garum and a little of the pasta water and plated. Lemon zest is grated on top, followed by a shower of grated *bottarga*. Pre-fried dehydrated capers (amazing) are then added, along with *mollica*, a mixture of breadcrumbs and dried ground anchovies.

When it was done, Tony and I shared the bowl of it right there at the stove.

Good God.

Simple. So simple.

Yet, sensorially stunning.

And for me, very comforting.

Were I ever to end up making a film for an extended period of time in Bagheria (fingers crossed), Tony Lo Coco would find me at his door every night of the week seeking comfort through his nourishment.

9

Doing a cooking show, or making a documentary about food for television, requires very particular talents, energies and skill sets, which I have been learning slowly over many years. Making a fictional narrative film in which food is the centre is another kettle of fish completely, and it was doing so (at times clumsily) that altered my life significantly.

I began writing what would eventually become the film *Big Night* over thirty years ago. I had always wanted to write a script that would be more in keeping with the tone and structure of a 'foreign film'. By this I mean a film that was primarily character driven, eschewed stereotypes, and ended somewhat ambiguously. When I lived on the Upper West Side in Manhattan during the 1980s, I was often unemployed for lengthy periods of time. In order to maintain sanity, instead of sitting at home and waiting for the phone to ring, I would exercise, visit museums, attend the theatre (affordable standing-room tickets only), or go to the cinema. Unlike today, there were many independently owned cinemas that showed foreign and independent films. One afternoon, in a little cinema on 68th Street and Broadway, which sadly is no longer there, after completing my daily workout, I ate an inexpensive, very unhealthy meal of something or other at the adjacent coffee shop (also no longer there), grabbed a cup of joe to go, paid my few dollars, and sat in a half-empty theatre to watch the glorious *Babette's Feast*.

If you haven't seen the film, I can only suggest that you do, especially if you're a 'foodie'. Not to spoil it, but to this day I vividly remember hearing the audience moan with never-to-be-realized pleasure as each dish was served in the climactic dinner scene. There is no doubt that the sounds that emanated from the cinema during *Babette's Feast* were echoed only in cinemas in the Times Square area that showed films of a very different ilk. (Or so I have been told.) At any rate, the subtle brilliance of the film and the communal experience of enjoying it stayed with me for many years afterwards and eventually became something of an inspiration for *Big Night*.

Any number of experiences can inspire or influence what anyone creates, but perhaps the primary inspiration for *Big Night* was an Italian restaurant in Miami that I had been to while filming early in my career that was owned by two immigrant brothers, one of whom would often sing as he served you. Although I cannot remember the brothers' names, or the name of the restaurant, I remember them as very charming raconteurs, and the food they made was delicious. During the same trip I also happened to meet a Corsican by the name of Pascal, who affected the air of a wannabe mafioso and owned another very successful Italian restaurant. This handsome, blue-eyed, foul-mouthed restaurateur became the template for the character of Pascal, played so perfectly in *Big Night* by Ian Holm. The brothers of the aforementioned eatery were the genesis of the characters Primo and Secondo, played by Tony Shalhoub and myself.

But there was one experience that I had as a very young man that is the reason the film is set in a restaurant at all. Between my sophomore and junior years of college it was my dream to work and live in Manhattan. Luckily, through familial generosity and good old nepotism, I was able to secure a position in a midtown restaurant called Alfredo's, the Original of Rome. My uncle Frank, my dad's brother, had designed the interior of Alfredo's and convinced the manager to give me a job, while my aunt Dora (my dad's sister) and her husband, Bob, were kind enough to house me in their spare bedroom in their beautiful East Side apartment. I could not have been more fortunate or happier. So, at age nineteen, I started work at Alfredo's as a busboy. But, because I spoke English or because I was a terrible busboy, or both, I was promoted to 'bar boy' almost straight away.

Alfredo's did a huge lunch business, mostly for businessmen who worked in the area or tourists who wanted a taste of authentic Italian food. I say 'authentic' because Alfredo's was a sister restaurant to the Alfredo's in Rome. The signature dish was, as you may have guessed, fettuccine Alfredo. This now-ubiquitous dish was created in 1907 by Alfredo di Lelio. It is basically fettuccine with butter and Parmigiano. Not basically; it actually is just that. But somehow, Alfredo's version, with a bit more butter and Parmigiano, as well as the spectacle of preparing it tableside, the long strands of fettuccine glistening with the fats of the butter and cheese, turned it and him into a worldwide sensation.

Sometime in the late 1970s, whoever owned the name saw an opportunity to open in New York, and the establishment is still in existence today, making their eponymous dish according to the original recipe. However, over the years, in many restaurants, the sublimely simple combination of butter and cheese has been altered to satisfy American palates. Cream has crept its way in (unnecessary), as well as chicken (yuck), broccoli (why?), and turkey (really? Fuck off). At any rate, fettucine Alfredo was basically all I ate for the entire summer, and as a college student, I thought it was just dandy.

Like most bartenders in most restaurants, at Alfredo's one not only made the drinks but poured the wine and made espresso and cappuccino. For about three hours it was a non-stop frenzy of dispensing liquids from one vessel to another as well as restocking the glasses, ice, fruit, garnishes, coffee beans, milk, etc. And I absolutely loved it. I not only find cleaning and organizing satisfying and relaxing, but they allow me time to ruminate on such questions as how I might approach a certain role or whether anyone will ever hire me again. I was therefore in OCD heaven scouring a bar, organizing a stockroom, and getting paid for it to boot.

Two different chain-smoking bartenders trained me. The first was a very fast-talking Albanian who, like many of his countrymen, also spoke Italian. The other was an American ex-marine, ex-mercenary soldier, and ex-convict who had spent time in prison for murder. (I think he was eventually released because his crime was deemed self-defence, or something like that. But he did actually kill someone either way, which, at the time, I thought was terrifyingly cool. Needless to say, I was very careful not to anger him.) So the murderous mercenary and the silver-tongued Albanian took me under their nicotine-stained wings and patiently taught me how to become a very fluid, efficient bartender, a skill I hope to regain, and to this day I am forever in their debt.

Like many restaurants, Alfredo's was a whirlwind of energy emanating from a cultural patchwork of employees. I must say, coming from the rather white suburbs of Westchester, it was a breath of fresh air to be a part of a place where the ethnic diversity of the staff rivalled that of the United Nations. Except for a couple of native New Yorkers, whose heritage I never came to know, the waiters were Greek, Egyptian, Italian, Albanian, Spanish and Eastern European, while most of the kitchen and bus staff were either Puerto Rican or Dominican (including the busboy Cristiano, whose name and parts of his personality were used for the waiter/busboy character in *Big Night*, played by the too-talented Marc Anthony). As a young actor, I revelled in the variety of accents and the accidental poetry that occurred when one person had to translate what they were thinking in one language in order to express it in another.

I was also particularly fascinated by how a restaurant's structure mirrored that of the theatre. The kitchen was 'backstage', which, during a lunch or dinner rush, was its own mad biosphere filled with frantic humans barely controlling flames and blades. Simultaneously, the dining room was 'onstage', where some of the same humans, after walking through a swinging door, instantaneously became cool, calm and collected, almost to the point of being benign. I have only ever witnessed this schizophrenic behaviour, and of course exhibited it myself, while performing in the theatre. It is as fascinating as it is disturbing, but in these venues it is not only normal but necessary.

Many years later, when I was finally able to make a living solely by acting and no longer needed to work in restaurants or paint apartments to survive, I began to mull over these experiences and decided to put them down in a form that vaguely resembled a screenplay. After a few years of getting nowhere fast, I asked my first cousin and one of my best friends, Joseph Tropiano, who loved cinema as much as I, to partner up. Over a period of the next five years or so, we eventually ended up with something that we were happy with. It was a screenplay that dramatized the struggle between commerce and art, portrayed the Italian immigrant as someone unconnected with the Mafia (a very unusual depiction in American cinema), showed the importance of food in Italian culture and how it is often used to express emotions, and did not have a happy ending. Little did we know we were making something that would be so well received or would become a 'food film' cult classic. If we had known any of that, we certainly would have negotiated a better back end.

━━━━━

I first met Isabella Rossellini through the co-director of *Big Night*, Campbell Scott. Isabella had committed to doing the film, while we shopped the script around to every producer in Christendom. I mentioned to Isabella that I would like to spend some time observing a chef at work and she introduced me to Pino Luongo, a restaurateur in New York City. After explaining what I was looking for, Pino suggested I go to Le Madri, unfortunately now defunct, one of his restaurants on 17th and Seventh Avenue, where Gianni Scappin was the head chef.

Gianni Scappin comes from the tiny village of Mason Vicentino in the Veneto region of northern Italy, where his family owned a small restaurant. After a brief stint in a seminary school as a young boy, Gianni realized he was not destined for the priesthood, and at the age of fourteen he began a four-year course at the Recoaro Terme Culinary Institute, which expanded his knowledge of Italian regional dishes. At the age of eighteen he moved to England and honed classic cooking skills in the French-influenced kitchen of the Dorset Hotel in Bournemouth. After a two-year obligatory stint in the Italian army in an Alpine skiing regiment, where he also cooked for his commanding officers (enlist me now), he worked at the famed Hotel Excelsior on the Lido in Venice. In the early 1980s he became the head chef at the very successful Castellano in New York for a few years until moving to New York's Bice (where he trained the late, great Anthony Bourdain) and finally to Le Madri. He eventually stepped away from the kitchen to oversee Pino Luongo's five New York restaurants. He left the city in 2000 to open up his own restaurants in upstate New York and taught at the Colavita Center for Italian Food and Wine at the CIA (that's the Culinary Institute of America, not the governmental spy organization).

Gianni could not have been more welcoming, and even though I had the option of visiting some of Pino's other kitchens, after meeting Gianni I never left Le Madri. Over the next couple of years, as we searched for funding for the film, whenever I wasn't working, I would spend time in Gianni's kitchen, learning everything I could from the staff and picking Gianni's brain. One of the things I asked Gianni to teach me was how to make a frittata because at the end of the film my character, Secondo, makes a frittata, which he shares with his brother, Primo, and the busboy/waiter, Cristiano. Our rather bold plan was to shoot the scene in one continuous take with no coverage. This meant that there would be no possibility of editing it down, and therefore every element would have to work perfectly, so I needed to be very adept at making it. Also, with the exception of a couple of lines at the beginning, there is no dialogue, so it almost felt like a scene from a silent film. Shooting the scene in a single wide master shot meant that I would have to cook the frittata in real time. If something went wrong, I would have to cut, reset, and begin another take.

We rehearsed a number of times to solidify the blocking of the actors and the basic timing of everything. During rehearsal I was using a pan that I had chosen from the prop master. Like all the props, it was or resembled a pan of the period, late 1950s, which meant there was no hope of slipping in a Teflon-coated pan to make my job a little easier. Needless to say, the frittata kept sticking to the pan and I started to panic, because if it didn't work seamlessly we would have to shoot coverage and end up editing the scene. Instinctively we all felt this would compromise the emotional integrity of the scene and rob it of its tension. So I grabbed a large aluminium pan and gave that a try, and luckily it worked perfectly every time. We ended up doing seven takes, two of which we had to abort partway through for reasons I can't remember, but the other five were 'keepers', as they say. I don't know which take we finally chose to use, but the entire scene is a single shot that lasts about five and a half minutes. I am so glad we were able to successfully shoot it as one continuous wide shot from beginning to end, as I believe it's what makes the scene so compelling. I still make frittatas all the time but they often end up sticking, no matter what pan I use, and I kick myself for not slipping that perfect pan into my bag on the last day of filming.

Here is a recipe for a frittata as taught to me by Gianni Scappin.

Frittata

– SERVES 2 –

5 or 6 large eggs
3 to 4 tablespoons olive oil
Sea salt
A good pinch of chopped fresh flat-leaf parsley (optional)
A good pinch of freshly grated Parmigiano-Reggiano
Freshly ground black pepper

- Crack the eggs into a bowl and beat them gently with a fork for a minute or so, making sure you angle the bowl so that you really blend them well. You could use a whisk instead of a fork, if you prefer, but you will end up with a puffier-textured frittata.

- In a 25cm sauté pan with sloping sides, heat the olive oil over medium-high heat. You want to get it pretty hot and tilt the pan to make sure the sides are well coated. When the oil is hot, season the eggs with salt and add the parsley, if using, then pour the mixture into the pan. Scramble the eggs vigorously with a silicone spatula, tipping and moving the pan continuously and drawing the egg from the sides into the middle. Keep the pan moving to make sure the eggs don't stick. Add the Parmigiano and a good grinding of pepper. Then flip or turn the frittata and cook for a minute or so more, until golden and cooked through. Serve immediately.

A couple of years later the same company that produced *Big Night* brought me to Rome for about five weeks to act in a film. My only friend in Rome at the time, Claudia Della Frattina, was working for a producer in a small office not far from where I was staying, and we got together for lunch the day after I arrived. I walked to her office thinking we would take a stroll and grab a bite, but we were in a slightly more residential area of the city, and when I arrived she said that she usually just ate in. I imagined she would have brought sandwiches like many people the world over, but there was no lunch box or takeaway bag on her desk. Instead I saw a small kitchen at one end of the office, to which a moment later Claudia was headed.

'I thought I might just cook for us,' she said in her beautifully accented English.

Let it be known that Claudia is very smart, very kind, and very pretty. She is half German, half Italian, with fair skin and large light blue eyes, and speaks English perfectly with a delicate Italian accent. She somehow eats pasta every day yet remains slender, is chic without spending absurd amounts on clothing, smokes hand-rolled cigarettes but never to excess, and loves to drink wine. Wisely, she no longer works in the film business; instead she designs hats and lives in Rome with her husband, a photographer who is even nicer than she is. In short, I want to be her. Or him. Or both of them.

Anyway, in response to her offer to cook for us, I said, 'Oh, don't go to any trouble.'

'It's no trouble. I make lunch most days anyway,' said she.

I first met Claudia during my first press junket for a Hollywood comedy that was great fun to make but, like many I've done, was a bomb at the box office. I was sent to do press in Italy and Spain in advance of the film's foreign release. Claudia was working freelance then and had been assigned to look after Kate and me during our stay in Rome, and we have remained friends ever since.

As we chatted about this and that, she filled a large pot with water and put it on the stove to boil. She then took two small *zucchine* and sliced them into thin rounds, and a clove of garlic, which she cut in half lengthwise. Pouring a glug of very dark green extra virgin olive oil into a pan, she dropped in the garlic along with a few pepperoncini. After they had simmered for a few minutes, she removed them, placed two handfuls of spaghetti in the now-boiling water, and began to sauté the *zucchine*. When the pasta was cooked, she strained it and mixed it together in the pan with some of the starchy pasta water.

With the exception of my father's Friday night specialty, *pasta con aglio e olio*, this might have been the simplest dish of pasta I'd ever eaten. The deeply flavoursome olive oil coated the sweet *zucchine*, helping it cling to the pasta, while just a suggestion of garlic emerged as the pepperoncini gave subtle heat to it all. Following my family's tradition, I had never really cooked with extra virgin olive oil – we used 'regular olive oil' (oil from olives that have been through many pressings, making it lighter but much less tasty) – nor did we ever use pepperoncini, as neither of my parents cared for anything spicy, so this unassuming dish was a bit of a revelation for me.

I know it sounds silly, but out of all the meals I have eaten it still remains one of my favourites. This is partly because it was cooked by and shared with my dear friend Claudia, but also because it was the perfect balance of five simple ingredients. As I travel, research and cook more over the years, I find this culinary equilibrium is realized with the most humble ingredients time and time again in the Italian kitchen. Even in a very small one in the back of an office in Rome many years ago.

A Pause for a Libation: The Old-Fashioned

Purportedly this legendary libation was created in 1806 in upstate New York and is the first drink to be called a 'cocktail'. Whiskey, bitters, sugar, water. That was basically it. By the middle part of that century the cocktail eventually became more and more complex, with the addition of a variety of liquors, like orange curaçao, absinthe, and who knows what else. Drinkers looking for the simpler version would ask for it to be made 'the old-fashioned way', hence its now-famous moniker. I am not a big bourbon drinker but this cocktail is very hard not to want.

Here's how to make it.

– SERVES 1 –

1 teaspoon simple syrup
A few dashes of Angostura bitters
2 shots of rye or bourbon
Ice
Orange slice and cherry, to garnish

• Pour the simple syrup into an 'old-fashioned glass', meaning a rocks glass.

• Add the Angostura bitters.

• Add the booze.

- Add the ice.

- Stir.

- Add the garnish.

- You could also make this with Scotch, or Irish whiskey if you prefer.

———————

A great drink for any season or reason.

10

Eating catered food on movie sets is often a terrifying prospect. Basically the way it works is, the bigger the budget, the better the food. When and for how long a lunch break is taken on any film is dictated by union rules, which differ from country to country. However, instead of taking a lunch break, which is the norm, I much prefer, as an actor as well as a director, to shoot 'continuous days', or what are called 'French hours'. This is also known as a 'running lunch', meaning that small plates of food or sandwiches are always available throughout the day, and a short break is taken about half-way through the day, where cast and crew can grab a quick bite or a little rest. I have always found that this makes the shooting day not only shorter but more efficient.

French hours are much more welcomed in England and in Europe but not as often in the United States, for reasons I have never fully understood. I know I am not writing a book about the machinations of the film industry, which would be even more tedious than this memoir, but it is important to know that food on set not only feeds people but also has a significant effect on the budget, the structure of a shooting day, and how a cast and crew work together successfully.

Now that you're about to nod off, here's a taste of how catering typically functions on most films.

———

When an actor arrives on set in the morning, which can sometimes be between four thirty and seven o'clock, depending on the complexity of the makeup, wardrobe or scene to be shot that day, a hot breakfast will be ready. The first people on set are the assistant directors, the runners, wardrobe, and hair and makeup. They will have already eaten or will be in the middle of their breakfast when the actor arrives. On a big-budget film, breakfast will be laid out on tables underneath a huge marquee. There will be steam trays of pre-fried eggs; scrambled eggs; pork, turkey or vegetarian sausages; bacon; hash browns; platters of smoked salmon; fruit; industrial toasters for toasting bagels; white bread; butter; jam; honey; yogurt; fruit juices; and urns of coffee and tea. If the budget is substantial and the producer appreciates their crew and how hard they work, there will also be an omelette station and then some. These are the kind of producers who also always employ a great craft service caterer who provides a table of savoury and sweet treats, and/or a truck making little sandwiches, smoothies, espresso, etc. to keep people well sated during potentially fifteen-hour days. Again, this is only on very large-budget films.

On most films there is one truck with a few beleaguered caterers doing their best with minimal funds to keep a cast and crew well fed and vaguely happy. The caterers, who are *actually* the first to arrive, at some ungodly hour, begin cooking two meals for a minimum of about fifty people every day. The quality of ingredients isn't usually of the highest calibre and their resources (and unfortunately often their talents) are stretched to the limit attempting to provide a variety of dishes every day for what could be up to an eight-week shoot.

In an effort to satisfy so many people, every lunch consists of a meat or chicken dish, a fish dish, two starches, two vegetables, a vegetarian dish, a salad or two, and dessert. This is not easy to do even on a healthy budget, and I don't envy their task. Unfortunately most caterers are not up to this task, which means that by the end of a film many people have stopped eating their food. Certain members of the cast and crew will end up bringing their own food if they have time to shop and prepare it, which isn't easy given the long and erratic working hours.

Usually when an actor arrives on set, they put in their breakfast order with the second AD (who runs the base camp where all the trailers are set up) and are then sent into hair and makeup to get ready. Many an actor in many a makeup chair has gobbled down many a breakfast as a poor makeup artist tries to daub foundation on a masticating jaw and bobbing Adam's apple while politely ignoring the sulphurous stench of the actor's hard-boiled eggs. It is also in the makeup trailer, an oasis of sorts for actors, where one can be assured of getting the best cup of coffee on set, because most makeup artists outfit them with good coffeemakers. However, just in case, I always bring at least two Nespresso machines the first day I start a job: one for the makeup trailer as a communal font of caffeine, and one for my own trailer, as I will often be trapped in there for hours on end and I want a good coffee when I want one.

As each country has its own cuisine, each film caterer in any given country will serve versions of its traditional dishes. Here are a few examples.

A Very English Breakfast: The UK

In my newly adopted home, fried eggs (often cooked in lard), sausages, bacon, baked or stewed or fried or steamed or whatever tomatoes (yuck), baked beans and porridge are a staple of every film-set breakfast. Sausage 'baps' are also always on offer. These are sliced brown or white buns layered with sausages (usually Cumberland) and sometimes an egg. The 'bap', meaning the bread, is usually rather dry and not very tasty, but if the sausage is of good quality this heart-stopping breakfast is hard to resist. I actually had to make a concerted effort to not eat one every morning working in England years ago because the project was to last almost five months and I thought if I continued wolfing them down, I might not live to complete the film.

There is not a great deal of importance put on craft services in

England, unless the budget is substantial and/or an American studio is producing the film. Otherwise all that is available is a 'tea table', tucked away in a corner of the set with an urn of hot water, a box or two of tea bags, milk, sugar, some paper cups, and a few packages of digestive biscuits. Wonderfully understated, almost quaint, and very British.

Anomalous Lunches: Italy

The first time I filmed in Italy, I was very excited because, well, as I have made abundantly clear, I love Italy. The film was based in Rome, where I was able to eat great meals every night and my days off. However, the catering on set was more than disappointing. For a nation that prioritizes food over just about everything and has informed the world's palate with its cuisine perhaps more than any other country, it puts no importance whatsoever on catered meals for films. I guess the reason for this is that, depending on location, whenever the cast and crew are able, they simply go out for lunch. Catering is always available for those crew members with limited time or an actor whose costume or makeup prohibits them from dining in public, but otherwise anyone who can eat elsewhere does so.

The only thing that makes Italian set catering bearable is that wine is always served. When one of the assistant directors asks an actor what they would like to eat for lunch, they simply say, 'White or red?' If the response is 'White', the actor will receive an entrée of chicken or fish. If it is 'Red', then red meat is served. These meals will be brought in a Styrofoam container with four compartments, one for the entrée; one for a starch, which is usually a pasta; and two for vegetables or possibly a salad, along with a small bottle of wine, the size you get on airplanes. To be fair, a lot of these meals are passable, but they're hardly inspiring, especially when one knows that close by, a plethora of brilliant restaurants are serving up some of the best food in the world. Yet, as disappointing as these lunches are, the on-set breakfasts are even worse.

Italians do not have a big breakfast culture. They don't eat eggs and meats like most of Europe, England and America, first thing in the morning. They have espresso or cappuccino but they prefer something sweet rather than savoury with which to start their day. The morning *caffe* will most likely be accompanied by a *cornetto* (a sweet croissant) or a *palmier*. In Rome pastries overflowing with obscene amounts of whipped cream or deep-fried cream-filled sugared doughnut-like sweets are often eaten. In Sicily, a brioche bun split open and filled with gobs of gelato is what passes for breakfast. I have tried all of them, and as I don't really have a sweet tooth or a death wish, I find them all rather unappetizing, especially first thing in the morning.

But breakfast on an Italian film set offers no such treats and brings the lack of interest in film catering to an even darker place. There is no catering truck. There is no toaster. There are no 'baps'. There is a table, on which sits a tray of low-grade supermarket *cornetti* and a smattering of small focaccia sandwiches containing a single slice of ham, prosciutto or salami. Beverages go no farther than a few cartons of warm orange juice and an urn of 'espresso' (or a thin and highly acidic version thereof), both of which are to be drunk out of flimsy plastic cups. If call time is after ten a.m., bottled beer is also served. That's it. Tragic for a country that is a culinary oracle.

Das Frühstück Fest: Germany

I have filmed in Germany only once, for about a week. The shots were mostly establishing exteriors, so the days were quite short; therefore my only experience with German film catering was the breakfasts, and they were extraordinary. I have never seen such a selection of meats, spreads, cheeses and breads anywhere except a farmers' market at Christmastime, and all of them were delicious. Someone please employ me there again.

Un Petit Déjeuner en Camion: France

We know that the French, like the Italians, are very particular about their cuisine. However, unlike the Italians, as we have just learned, on film sets they retain their appreciation of food and its presentation. I have written about how a lunch hour can really slow down a day on set, if not just protract it. This is not so in France. A lunch hour is religiously observed, and the days seldom go over the allotted time. If they do, I have heard stories of crews just going home. It's that simple. And frankly (no pun intended), I raise my hat to them, because most film sets are exercises in disorganization, miscommunication and inefficiency resulting in unnecessarily long days for everyone.

I spent a week observing Robert Altman (who was very efficient) direct *Prêt-à-Porter* in Paris many years ago. The location was a ritzy hotel in the centre of Paris that was standing in for a ritzy hotel in the centre of Paris. When lunch was called, everyone was directed down to the street, where a white eighteen-wheeler was parked. A steel stairway led into the back of the truck, which was outfitted with rows of tables on either side, creating an aisle in the middle. Each table could seat four to six people and was covered in a white tablecloth. On every table sat bottles of still and sparkling water, water glasses, wine glasses, salt and pepper shakers, cutlery, cloth napkins and a bottle of red wine. A small team of waiters dressed in white shirts and vests welcomed us in, and a moment later one of them was at our table listing two or three options for that day's lunch. Having made our decisions, the waiter poured red wine for those who wanted it and was off to get a bottle of cold white for the others.

I was flabbergasted, as it was a distant scream from any catering I had experienced on any film set. I couldn't help but stare in disbelief at the cast and crew eating together inside a truck so elegantly appointed, while gay Paree buzzed away around us. The whole thing was so wonderful, civilized and strange that there is a part of me that thinks perhaps I may have just dreamed it all. If so, I'd like to dream it again on every film I make from now on.

Cold Comfort: Iceland

About six years ago, I was fortunate enough to film a British television show called *Fortitude*. I was very excited to be asked because I thought it was an interesting project; I knew I'd be working with two extraordinary actors, Michael Gambon and Sofie Gråbøl; and I'd be able to shoot mostly at home in London but also in Iceland, a country I've always wanted to visit. I don't know why, but I have always been drawn to northern climes much more than to warmer parts of the world. I find the redundant sunshine of southern California mind-numbing, the humidity of the American South loathsome, and the tropics make me want to curl up into a ball and die before I drown in my own sweat.

No, for some unknown reason, I feel more at home in the Italian Alps than I do in the brutal heat of Puglia. I like brisk autumns, snowy winters, rainy springs and temperate summers. The change of seasons allows for a change in one's wardrobe (I'm sartorially obsessed) and, most important, one's diet. A *boeuf carbonnade* tastes a thousand times better in the last days of autumn than when it's eighty degrees and the sun is shining. An Armagnac is the perfect complement to a snowy night by the fire but not to an August beach outing, just as a crisp Orvieto served with *spaghetti con vongole* is ideal 'al fresco' on a sunny summer afternoon but not nearly as satisfying when eaten indoors on a cold winter's night. One thing feeds the other. (Pun intended.) So a visit to Iceland to escape the gloom of what is known in London as 'winter' was an exciting prospect.

However, my greatest concern, as you can probably guess, if you're still reading this, was the food.

We were to be staying about an hour's flight away from Reykjavík in a little town of about 2,300 people called Egilsstaðir. As I've said, I don't eat dairy and eat very little sugar, but at this point I had also cut gluten out of my diet, so I was rather nervous about just what exactly I'd be able to eat while I was there. Our hotel rooms had no kitchens, so I knew I'd be beholden to whatever was served in house or at the few restaurants in town. I was to be there for almost two weeks, so I brought a box of canned soups, gluten-free crackers, and a lot of other pathetic free-of-this and free-of-that foodstuffs.

I checked into our Icelandair Hotel, which was the tallest building around, at five stories, and a study in boxy nondescript minimalism. The ground floor consisted of a small check-in desk to the left of which was a little seating area and a bar. Beyond the bar was a very spartan dining room. Although the place was clean and well lit and the staff rather cheery, I thought that two weeks here might be pushing it. My room was very much the same, actually less than spartan. (Which, I guess would be just . . . spart?) There was a firm bed (and I mean firm), a small closet, a dresser, a desk, a small fridge, a kettle, a bathroom, and a television that, when it worked, got four channels, one of which was BBC One, thank God. In short, it's a perfect hotel if you are in the witness protection programme. I sighed. Loudly. But in Iccland, no one can hear you sigh.

I unpacked and hopped into the shower, which, seconds later, I learned offered only sulphurous water. After dressing and hoping I didn't smell like a rotting egg, I headed downstairs to get a drink and a bite to eat. I met some of my colleagues at the bar and we chatted about the 'eggy' water, how beautiful Iceland seemed, and things work related. After a couple of cocktails we made our way into the dining room.

The wine list was as minimal as the decor but there were some very drinkable choices, which was fine with me as I am not one for long lists of fancy overpriced wines. The menu had a few appetizers, about five entrées, a few sides, and salads, all of which looked very promising. Most notably one of the appetizers was fresh langoustine that I was told came from nearby waters. I asked about the lamb, which they said was locally raised. My decision made, I ordered both dishes and a green salad with fresh tomatoes.

Soon our appetizers arrived and on my plate sat two beautiful langoustines. They were split down the middle, grilled lightly, and dressed with parsley butter. In short, they were perfect. Because langoustines are quite delicate they must be grilled quickly and gently. I find that they are often grilled for too long and lose their moisture, as they have no fat. At the same time the taste of the grill itself can overwhelm the sweetness of the flesh and the whole point of them is eradicated. These were perfect. The salad that followed was of light green lettuce leaves and bright red cherry tomatoes with a chive vinaigrette. I was stunned. How were they able to get produce this fresh in the middle of nowhere? My lamb arrived next, and to this day it is the best lamb I have ever eaten. Perfectly cooked with a slight char on the outside, soft and pink in the centre, had a salty sweetness, and melted in your mouth.

I asked our waitress where the fresh vegetables had come from. She told me they were locally grown without pesticides in geothermal-powered greenhouses.* Were they as sweet and deeply flavoured as those from southern Italy? No, they were very different, but they popped when you bit them and were delicious in their own right. Regarding the unforgettable lamb, I was to discover a couple of days later that Icelandic sheep feed on the low grass and herbs that compose most of the island's flora as well as seaweed, thus imparting to them their distinctive flavour.

From then on I looked forward to dinner at our ascetic little hotel. Luckily most of the cast loved to eat and drink, and this became the first of many nights we would spend together doing just those two things as Michael Gambon regaled us in his sonorous baritone with hilarious stories of a chequered life in theatre and film.

One beautiful sunny morning we drove about forty-five minutes inland to a more mountainous part of the island, where we were to film that day. As we drove along the roads the snow became deeper and deeper until we were driving between two fifteen-foot-high walls of the stuff. The only two actors filming that day were Michael

---

* Ninety-nine per cent of Iceland's energy is from renewable sources. Up until about twenty years ago most vegetables were imported, but now at least half are grown on the island, mostly in geothermal greenhouses.

Gambon and myself, so no makeup or wardrobe trailers were necessary, and even if they were, there would have been no place to park them. We dressed and were made up in our small individual trailers, which were parked below base camp perilously close to a waterfall and a torrent of a river. When all was ready we were ferried up to location, in a special vehicle capable of climbing over and through substantial mounds of snow. We reached base camp and were then brought by skimobile farther up the glacier to the set. As I love winter and all that comes with it, I was in heaven. We shot some of the scene, and when it was time for lunch we were Ski-Dooed back down to base camp.

As there was no room anywhere for a catering truck, there was a small pop-up tent from which the food would be served that day. Inside were our usual friendly caterers, whom we all agreed had done an excellent job so far. Today they stood over two huge pots perched on top of gas burners. I peered inside, and bubbling away was some kind of wonderfully aromatic stew. Unlike most days, when they had served us a variety of dishes in our production office, a fish factory the producers had commandeered in a small town where most of our filming took place, this single dish was to be our meal for the day due to the geographic limitations of the location. We grabbed our plastic bowls and queued up for what I was soon to learn was the traditional Icelandic stew known as *kjötsúpa*. My bowl filled, I grabbed a piece of bread, walked back out into the blinding sunlight, plopped myself down in a snowbank with my colleagues, and tucked in. All I can say is that I don't know if it was the surroundings, the camaraderie that extreme and remote locations engender, or the fact that the caterers served their historic stew with such nationalistic pride, but it was a brilliant meal.

Kjötsúpa is a traditional rustic Icelandic dish that is somewhere between a soup and a stew. It is made with inexpensive cuts of lamb or mutton that are cubed and then boiled along with the bone for about forty-five minutes or so. After the meat has broken down, root vegetables such as carrots, potatoes, swedes, turnips, onions, etc. are added, as well as stock, some dried herbs, maybe some cabbage, and the whole thing is then cooked for another twenty minutes or so. Sometimes oats or rice are added to thicken it.

Let's face it, most stews are basically all made the same way. Sometimes the meat is browned first, maybe a mirepoix is sautéd, and then everything is put together in a pot. Once you know how thin or thick you like it and what other ingredients you fancy, you can just kind of make a stew up as you go along. Grab a not-very-fancy piece of meat, the fresh or fading vegetables from the fridge, some wine, stock, herbs, etc., etc., and knock yourself out. (I have only recently started cooking stews and stocks in a pressure cooker, and it has changed my life. I don't know what took me so long.) Along with good bread or served with polenta, noodles or rice, a stew is quick, hearty, inexpensive and comforting. In summer, I often make fish stews like *cacciucco* or some variation thereof because I love the idea of bringing simple ingredients together in one huge pot and presenting it like some sort of religious offering to whatever deities are seated at my table that day.

Anyway, this *kjötsúpa* was so superb that I embarrassed myself by going back for thirds. To this day it remains the best catered meal I have eaten on any film set from the South Pole to the Arctic Circle and all points in between.

———

Due to the limited number of flights from Reykjavík to London, flying back home often required an overnight stay in the island's capital city. With the exception of a small percentage of older buildings, the architecture is minimalistic. The houses are simple boxlike structures with roofs or even walls of corrugated metal, most of which are painted bright, cheery colours. It's a small city to say the least, yet it's the most populated in the country with about 125,000 people. (On the entire island there are only a little over 350,000 inhabitants.) On one trip home I was not able to make the last flight to London so I had to spend the night in Reykjavík, as did Michael Gambon and the wonderful actor Darren Boyd. I had asked a number of people about what restaurants they'd recommend in the capital and I was consistently told to visit Grillmarkaðurinn. Although it was a busy place, I was fortunately able to get a reservation for the three of us that night.

Grillmarkaðurinn is a rather hip upscale eatery that serves mostly meats. (They also have a sister restaurant called Fiskmarkaðurinn that obviously serves mostly fish.) The menu lists dishes such as heavily marbled rib-eyes, tomahawk steaks, and tenderloin of horse. I don't remember horse being on the menu when I was there; if it had been, I would have ordered it, because I have always wanted to try it. It is frequently eaten in France and Italy, yet I have never ventured to order it or buy it when I am there. I can only assume my trepidation stems from the fact that I once owned a couple of horses. My late wife, Kate, was an avid rider, as were my kids for a few years when they were young, and it feels too close to eating one's pet, not out of desperation but just because one can. At any rate, Grillmarkaðurinn's menu also listed two items I'd not seen in any restaurant before, minke whale and puffin. I was intrigued and so I inquired. The waiter assured me that the minke whale, which is indigenous to the Icelandic waters, was not endangered and was procured in a sustainable fashion, and that the same was true of the puffin. My guilt vaguely assuaged, I ordered both.

When my plate of whale arrived I thought the waiter had mistaken my order, because what was before me looked like crimson medallions of beef. He assured me it was indeed whale and so I dived in. The flesh was seared quickly like one would do with a piece of fresh tuna and maybe flavoured with a little olive oil and salt, but I can't be sure. All I know is that the flavour was rich and deep, like a Kobe steak but more complex because it also had the delicate fishiness of sushi-grade tuna. Never had vaguely assuaged guilt tasted so good. The puffin was next, which was just the breast meat, smoked and sliced. To me, the smoking had dried it out to the point where it almost could have been the breast of any small, cute bird we probably shouldn't kill, but this is not to say that it wasn't very tasty. However, unlike the whale, I wouldn't rush to order it again. Although placing an order for minke these days might be to no avail, as I have recently read that Iceland is putting a halt to their whaling since demand for the meat is declining. It seems they can make more money from tourists who are keen to pay a pretty króna to *watch* whales rather than *ingest* them, which in the end is probably not such a bad thing. I do not know about the fate of the flamboyantly beaked puffin, however. As far as I know they are still culled for the smoker and the plate, but since there are over eight million of them on an island of less than a half a million people, most of whom aren't very interested in eating them anyway, I'm not going to stay awake nights worrying.

Truth be told, I don't really remember what else we ate that night as many a Martini and much wine was had, but I do remember leaving Grillmarkaðurinn more than sated, happy that I had tasted two new dishes, and wishing I'd had another few nights in town.

I was so thrilled that when it came to eating well in Iceland my original concerns were completely unfounded, and also embarrassed that they were unfairly prejudiced by my ignorance. I thought I would be subjected to *skyr* and fermented shark at every meal, when in fact my Icelandic culinary experience was very much the opposite; it was a revelation.

11

Robert Altman was an extraordinary film director and producer who made a number of brilliant and influential films throughout his fifty-year career, *M*A*S*H*, *Nashville* and *Gosford Park* being just a few. Bob had produced an Alan Rudolph film that Campbell Scott was working on along with a few other friends of mine in Montreal. Campbell and I had teamed up to co-direct *Big Night* and would meet periodically to discuss in what style we might shoot the film if ever we got the money to actually make it. While he was filming Alan's movie, Campbell suggested I visit the set, as he thought that I would like the way it was being shot. Kate and I visited for a weekend, saw some friends, and observed the process. Alan asked me to return in a couple of weeks to play a small role, which I was more than happy to do. After this Campbell and I approached Altman to see if he would produce our film and help shepherd it through the complex process of raising the money. We thought that having someone of his stature and talent would help two first-time directors get a foot into the tightly closed doors of Hollywood. After reading the script and meeting with us, he agreed to lend a hand to that foot.*

Although he was quite busy, Bob was very generous with his time, and when I told him I'd like to shadow him on set, he was more than welcoming. Soon afterwards, I arrived in Paris for a week to observe Bob direct *Prêt-à-Porter*. The cast of the film was a who's who of mainstream, independent and foreign film actors, a few of whom were my friends. It was quite thrilling for me to watch Bob work in his usual relaxed but very singular way and get to meet some of my favourite actors, like Sophia Loren and Marcello Mastroianni.

One afternoon when those two icons were filming a scene, they wanted to impart something to Altman, but because of the language barrier it was proving impossible. Since I spoke some Italian, I became a translator of sorts, and by hook or by crook, the issue was solved. After filming that day, Mastroianni approached me and asked if I would like to join him and the producer Jon Kilik for dinner. Marcello Mastroianni was and remains one of my all-time acting heroes. Besides the fact that he was painfully handsome and debonair, his performances ranged from the powerfully moving to the delicately comic. I must admit even the birth of my children has not given me the joy I felt from that invitation. All right, the kids'

---

* Bob Altman did what he could to help us bring *Big Night* to fruition, including making an announcement at Cannes one year that he was producing a film called 'Pasta Fazool'. Because he hated the title *Big Night*, he came up with this terrible title, which I think probably did more harm than good. However, although he never ended up seeing the film through as a producer, we remained friends until his death.

entry into the world comes first, but by a nose. Literally. Anyway, when Mr Mastroianni wrote down the name of the restaurant with a shaky cigarette-stained hand on a torn slip of paper and gave it to me, I think I bowed like a geisha in thanks.

———

At eight p.m., after having a drink or two to steady my nerves, a little Dutch courage as it were, I meet Jon and Marcello at an Italian restaurant called Romano's. It is a small, homey place run by an Italian whose name I believe is actually Romano. Marcello explains that this is one of his regular haunts and that the food is wonderful. Romano comes to the table and offers us a drink. Marcello orders a Scotch on the rocks, 'to open up the stomach', he explains in his broken English. This is a very Italian tradition and belief and where the term *aperitivo* comes from: '*aprire*', 'to open', '*tivo*', a colloquial shortening of '*appetito*'; hence, 'to open the appetite'. Jon and I of course order the same thing. We chat for a bit, which is slow going as Jon speaks no Italian, Marcello speaks only broken English, and I am so nervous I am butchering *both* languages. Soon Romano returns and asks what we would like to eat, for as far as I remember we were never given a menu. He and Marcello confer quasi-conspiratorially but loud enough for us to hear.

Their exchange goes something like this:

ROMANO: Allora, che mangiamo sta sera?

MARCELLO: Non so. Forse . . . Posso avere un po di pasta fagioli?

ROMANO: Ma, certo.

Marcello looks to us, wondering if we would like the same. Jon understands 'pasta fagioli' so there is no need to translate. We both nod in hearty agreement.

ROMANO: Perfetto. Tre fagio – E poi?

MARCELLO: Umm . . . ?

Marcello is unsure as to what he would like. He's so human.

ROMANO: Forse un po d'agnello.

MARCELLO: Cotelette?

ROMANO: Si. Dolcissimi. Lo faccio semplice, olio, vino bianco, aglio, sale, rosemarino.

MARCELLO: Perfetto.

Marcello turns to us to see if that is suitable. Jon is confused. I translate.

ME: Lamb chops with olive oil, white wine, garlic, salt and rosemary.

JON: Sounds great.

I turn to my new friend Marcello.

ME: Perfetto. Grazie.

MARCELLO: Allora.

ROMANO: Perfetto. Tre cotolette.

Exit Romano.

After our drinks a carafe of red house wine is brought to the table, which I nervously swill, Jon sips, and Marcello waters down as per doctor's orders. The *pasta fagioli* arrives and it is an absolutely delicious creamy bowl of what I remember being a mix of cannellini and borlotti beans with a short pasta. It is very comforting and reminds me of something my grandmother would make.

Soon after, the lamb chops arrive, and as per Romano's description, they are small and sweet and cooked perfectly. They need nothing more than just a touch of the few ingredients to make them mouth-wateringly good. There was probably a salad and some kind of vegetable but I cannot recollect them. However, I do remember after the wine and the delicious food my translating skills improved, or at least I imagined they did, and I was finally a bit more at ease dining with one of the people I admired most in the world.

After dinner Marcello ordered a *digestivo*. This consisted of a half shot of amaro and a half shot of Fernet-Branca. Jon and I naturally ordered the same. I introduced it to my father and it is still something we drink together to this day. We have of course named it after my oldest and closest friend. Yes, it is called a Marcello.

The next day I told my friends on the film not only how lovely the evening was but also that I had discovered a wonderful, authentic

Italian restaurant. A few nights later we all gathered around a table at Romano's, more than ready for a great meal. However, when the food came there was little about it that resembled anything vaguely related to Italian cuisine. I should have known I was going to be disappointed when I asked the waiter if they had *pasta fagioli* and he looked at me as if I were mad. I ordered a piece of salmon, which I imagined would be cooked as simply as the lamb chops I had shared just the other night with my best friend in the world, Marcello Mastroianni. Instead I was presented with an overbaked slice of fish that was swimming in cream and covered with a carapace of cheese. Looking at the dishes my friends had ordered, I realized that they were all versions of Italian recipes altered to satisfy the most base of Parisian tastes. It seems that Romano's stayed in business catering to their clientele's questionable palates even if it meant denying the delicate, delicious simplicity of their native recipes. Although this is very common (it is in fact the primary plot device in *Big Night*), and it's understandable that restaurants do have to make a living, it is always sad to know that in kitchens everywhere around the world many talented chefs are reining in the culinary gifts they have learned from their families in order to accommodate what is the mediocrity of the status quo.

Obviously I never returned to Romano's, and as far as I can tell they are no longer in business. Sadly, I never saw Marcello Mastroianni again, but I still have the memory of that wonderful night and the piece of paper on which he penned the restaurant's address, which, as stated in my will, is to be buried with me.

12

Making Nora Ephron's film *Julie and Julia* and playing Julia Child's husband, Paul, to Meryl's Julia was an honour and a pleasure. As I've said, from an early age I was enamoured of Julia Child and therefore more than keen to enter the world that Nora so lovingly realized. For certain projects a lot of research is necessary, but it is not always as enjoyable as it was this time around. In this case, I read as much as possible about Julia and Paul, spent time with Paul's great-nephew, the wonderful writer Alex Prud'homme, and, to get a real taste of his life (pun intended and achieved), cooked a number of recipes from my copy of Julia's *Mastering the Art of French Cooking* that my mother had given me years ago. (In fact, Meryl and I made *blanquette de veau* together for Kate and our friend Wren Arthur one night, which surprisingly turned out very well. Although due to disorganization and poor planning, we served dinner two hours later than intended. I blame the star of the film.)

Paul Child was a fascinating man. He was an expert in judo, a painter and a photographer (although he only had the use of one eye due to a childhood accident); spoke fluent French; worked in the OSS (the precursor to the CIA) in Sri Lanka, where he met Julia; and eventually became a member of the American diplomatic corps after the Second World War, working as a cultural liaison in France, Germany and Norway. He was as voracious a reader as he was an eater, and therefore had an extensive knowledge of countless subjects. During their time abroad Paul encouraged Julia to study cooking and eventually take those skills to television when they returned to live in the US, in the early 1960s. Retired at this point, he supported her behind the scenes, carrying her kitchen kit from studio to studio, helping with prep work, and washing pots and pans at the end of the day as well as illustrating and taking photos for her cookbooks. In short, he was a very advanced fella for his time and one of the most interesting people I've had the pleasure of playing. The entire experience was only made better by Nora, Meryl and the convivial atmosphere on set. As I may have alluded to in previous pages, this is a rather rare occurrence.

That conviviality remained when we were reunited over a year later for our press tour. To kick it off, President and Michelle Obama chose *Julie and Julia* to be the first film shown in the White House screening room when he was first elected, an event to which we were all thrilled to be invited. When we arrived, the president and the First Lady greeted us and could not have been more charming as we tried our best not to gush all over them. After a little chitchat, President Obama left to attend to some affair of some state while Mrs Obama and the rest of us went to the small White House screening room to watch the film. We knew in that moment that no matter where we subsequently went on the remainder of the press tour, this would be a tough act to follow. However, there was one other experience that was also very notable, but for distinctly different reasons.

There's a little restaurant slightly inland from the Normandy coast, the name of which I can't remember, and that's probably a good thing. This is where Meryl, Chris Messina and I found ourselves one afternoon as we were heading from Deauville to Paris. We had been promoting *Julie and Julia* at the Deauville film festival, which is one of my favourites because it is a very relaxed affair, unlike most of the other major festivals. At Deauville there is a fair amount of the usual repetitive press interviews to be done as well as a few photo shoots (always painful), but screenings take place only during the day, hence the evenings and nights are for the most part one's own. Guests will stay at the Hôtel Barrière Le Royal, with a view of the seemingly endless beaches made famous by the painter Boudin over a century ago. The air is fresh; the skies are blue until they suddenly turn a deep grey and let loose a dramatic thunderstorm, making the whole experience quite romantic. The festival and the setting are a film lover's and a filmmaker's dream. The location is a food lover's dream.

That area of the Gallic coast is of course known for its seafood as well as its more rustic country fare. The buffet lunch poolside at the Hôtel Le Royal is in itself a typical Norman treat. Platters of *fruits de mer* on beds of ice, crisp green salads with a classic shallot dressing, fresh baguettes, and bottles of rosé or Sancerre are on offer and quickly snapped up by all the guests. There are also many wonderful restaurants in the surrounding area if one is interested in venturing out of the Barrière bubble.

I have been to the festival often over the years, staying for varying lengths of time, but on this trip I was there only a couple of days as we were scheduled to attend a premiere for the film and a press junket in Paris. The morning of our departure saw us in a parade of cars heading northward to our destination with a small detour to the hallowed beaches of D-Day. As a World War II buff, I was beyond excited to visit this place I had read so much about. Needless to say it turned out to be more fascinating and moving than I ever could have imagined, and years later I am still overwhelmed by the experience.

After our tour (well, actually Meryl got the tour; our designated guide, who was I think the head of the whole site, was clearly smitten and hastily whisked her away while the rest of us tried to keep up as best we could, straining to overhear a fact or two that he imparted breathily into my co-star's ear), we returned to our convoy and headed for lunch at a little country bistro that one of the drivers was familiar with.

We arrived at a charming eatery off a side road famished and thirsty for the grape as usual. The cast of characters at the table was composed of M. Streep; my publicist Jenn; Chris Messina; Meryl's brother Dana, an avid eater to say the least; and myself. The owner, who was no doubt as excited to meet Meryl as our D-Day beach tour guide, at least had the decency to acknowledge the presence of her dining companions, and swiftly brought us bread, water, the menu, and, thankfully, wine.

As I said, we were starving, but we also knew that we were going to Paris, where we would end up eating a lot of something somewhere wonderful, so we all vowed to be judicious with our lunch orders. The menu consisted of mostly dishes from the area and was primarily more meat and game than fish based. There were, of course, eggs mayonnaise, mâche salad as a starter, and entrées like *onglet, omelette aux herbes*, or *tripes à la mode de Caen*. Perusing the menu, I noticed that a specialty of the house was *andouillette*. I thought it looked interesting and asked Meryl if she had ever eaten it. She said she hadn't, but since we both expressed a penchant for andouille sausages we figured this must be a diminutive version of them given that the name ended in '*ette*'. When the charming owner and waitress returned we ordered our starters (and more wine, as it had obviously evaporated in the afternoon heat) and inquired about the *andouillette*. They explained that it was a sausage, to which we said of course we knew as much (being careful not to make too much a show of our worldliness), and that it was particular to Normandy. Wanting to demonstrate that the 'ugly American' is an endangered species, all of us, with the exception of Jenn, ordered the *andouillette* with definitive gusto accompanied by a kind of 'Bring it on!' sweeping gesture of the arm.

Our host noted our order and gracefully made his exit. A moment later the waitress arrived with our wine. Corks popping, we chatted about the experience of the festival and how lucky we had been to have a private tour of the D-Day memorial site, or at least follow

Meryl's private tour. Our starters arrived, over which we yummed and ahhhed, while we ordered more wine because . . . well, there was none left in the bottles because I guess we drank it. We ate heartily as the waitress topped us up, and before we knew it we had finished our first course.

After a few minutes' rest our entrées arrived. Jenn's bright green salad was placed before her, but laid before the rest of us was a plate upon which sat something that I can only say bore a staggering resemblance to a horse cock. I watched Meryl's face drop slightly and from her mouth come a small, 'Oh.' She then smiled politely and glanced at me, searching for an answer to a question yet unformed, but seeing that I was staring at the contents of my plate with slack-jawed confusion, she turned back to the waitress.

MERYL: Is this the . . . um . . . ?

WAITRESS: *Oui, madame,* the *andouillette.*

MERYL: Oh, good. I wasn't . . . I thought . . . um . . . *Merci.*

WAITRESS: *Merci beaucoup, madame.*

Placing the remaining plates of this Norman specialty in front of Dana and Chris's empty chair (he had gone to make a phone call), the waitress departed with a cheery, '*Bon appétit!*'

There was a moment of silence. Not for the fallen on the beaches we had just visited but for fear of what was before us. We exchanged concerned looks. I spoke first.

TASTE

ME: Huh. This is not what I . . .

MERYL: No . . . Not at all.

Dana stared at his while stubbing out a cigarette.

DANA: It's supposed to be good. That's what they said. Right?

ME: Yeah, but . . . I thought it would be . . .

DANA: What?

ME: Well, smaller. You know, 'ette'. *Andouill*ette. Small.

MERYL: Yes, me too. I mean this is . . .

ME: Well, it looks like a fucking horse cock.

MERYL: Yes, it certainly does.

A beat of silence.

MERYL: Oh well.

She cut off a small piece and placed it in her mouth. She chewed gingerly. Her face showed a lifetime of human emotion in a split second. She swallowed. She brought her napkin to her lips. She spoke very quietly.

MERYL: Well . . . it does have a bit of the barnyard about it.

I placed a tidbit into my mouth and before it had passed my second

193

taste bud I was spewing it out on to my plate and trying not to projectile-vomit the accumulation of two gluttonous days all over my colleagues. I grabbed my wine, swilled it, stuffed half a baguette into my mouth, and chased it down with more wine. To my right, I could see that Dana had tucked into the thing wholeheartedly and seemed to be doing fine until he was halfway through his second forkful, when he suddenly looked at me, his eyes wide with terror. Grabbing his napkin, he ejected the remnants into it and said something like, 'EErgaarhhuergh! Christ!'

At this moment Chris Messina returned to the table and eyed his awaiting entrée. As he took his seat all three of us shouted:

ALL THREE: Don't touch that!

CHRIS: Why? Is it –

ALL THREE: Just don't. Don't.

The waitress came by and asked if everything was all right and we assured her that it was. I even went so far as to praise the dish but noticed a slight smirk on her lips as she departed. Moments later the owner returned and looked at us bemusedly.

OWNER: The *andouillette*. It is not . . .

ALL FOUR OF US: Yes, I mean it's great, but it's just not what we were expecting. It's a little different than others we've had . . .

As more pathetic excuses and untruths were spoken, he smiled and nodded understandingly. After a moment he told the waitress, who had been lurking behind him, more than amused, to clear our plates and asked us if we would like to order anything else.

ALL FOUR OF US: Four omelettes, please.

OWNER: Will that be all?

ALL FOUR OF US: And more wine.

As we waited for our assuredly benign entrées to arrive, we decided that it was not only the brave Allied forces that caused the Germans to pull back. Most likely it was the fear of having to eat *andouillette* day after day as penance for their brutal conquest of Normandy that also precipitated the Nazi retreat.

Here is the objective, very politically correct Wikipedia definition of *andouillette*.

Andouillette (French pronunciation: [ãdujɛt]) is a coarse-grained sausage made with pork (or occasionally veal), chitterlings (intestine), pepper, wine, onions and seasonings. Tripe, which is the stomach lining of a cow, is sometimes an ingredient in the filler of an andouillette, but it is not the casing or the key to its manufacture. True andouillette will be an oblong tube. If made with the small intestine, it is a plump sausage generally about 25mm in diameter but often it is much larger, possibly 7–10cm in diameter, and stronger in scent when the colon is used. True andouillette is rarely seen outside France and has a strong, distinctive odour related to its intestinal origins and components. Although sometimes repellent to the uninitiated, this aspect of andouillette is prized by its devotees.

Need I say more?

13

I have heard that Edward G. Robinson would do three films a year, one for love, one for money, and one for location. Some day I hope to be in a position to be that choosy. There are a number of questions I ask when I am offered a job as an actor. Who's directing? Who's in it? How long will I be needed? How much money? Where does it shoot? But the last question, location, is a really crucial one. I do my best to find interesting and/or lucrative work close to home as often as possible, because in over thirty-eight years in this business we call 'show', I have acquired more air miles than I would like to remember flying between locations and home so as not to be away from my family for long stretches of time. For this reason obviously the farther away the location, the more I grapple with the choice. The other reason is the food.

If the project is filming in Europe, the choice is pretty simple, as good food is plentiful and frequent trips home are easily done. If I am offered a job across the Atlantic, say, in Toronto, Vancouver or

Montreal, even though I'm aware the 'commute' will be exhausting, I know I will be in cities that are home to a plethora of great restaurants and food shopping. I mention these cities because for many years now countless television shows and films have been shot there. Most people think that Los Angeles is the home of filmmaking, but Canada and England are now the meccas of cinema production. This suits me just fine as I love Canada, I live in London, and I hate LA. For instance, I know that in Vancouver I'll be able to eat amazing Chinese or Japanese food, explore the great homegrown restaurants that spring up every year, and find great fresh seafood, meat and produce to cook myself. I know also that my first stop will be my favourite restaurant, Cioppino's in Yaletown, run by chef Pino Posteraro and his brother Celestino.

I first visited Cioppino's about twenty years ago when I was making a film for which I was well paid and which no one should ever see. Pino and Celestino, who, like my family, hail from Calabria, treated me like a brother from the moment I entered their restaurant. When Kate, our two-year-old twins, our one-month-old, and my parents came to stay with me, we would eat there whenever we could because the brothers created the warm atmosphere of an Italian home on a Sunday afternoon. Even though twenty years have passed, Pino, Celestino and I have remained friends. But it is not this friendship that prompts me to say that Cioppino's is one of the best restaurants I have ever eaten in. It's the food.

Coming from an aristocratic Calabrese family, Pino learned the basics of cooking from his mother, who herself had studied with professional chefs. He worked with Armando Zanetti, the two-star Michelin chef, in Turin, after which he became chef de cuisine in Ristorante Bologna at the Mandarin hotel in Singapore. The mid-nineties found him and his young family in Vancouver, where he had been offered the job of head chef at the famous Il Giardino. Soon afterwards he teamed up with his brother Celestino, who had owned his own successful restaurants over the years, and they opened Cioppino's. Pino's ability to combine the many facets of his culinary education and experiences has allowed him to create dishes that take Italian cooking to another level. His expert use of the sous-vide method of cooking alone, especially twenty years ago when he first opened, sets him apart from so many chefs, as does his ability to integrate Asian flavours and techniques into Italian dishes.

Whenever I'm working in Vancouver, I am more than excited to see Pino and Celestino and dine at their restaurant. While on set, I find myself constantly asking the assistant director, who basically controls the schedule of a shooting day, what time I will wrap, so I can be sure to get to Cioppino's before it closes. (This is really what most actors are thinking when they are, well . . . acting.) When I was filming there last year I came to Cioppino's one night straight from work exhausted and famished. The brothers warmly welcomed me, and within moments there was a glass of wine in my hand and the question 'What would you like to eat?' had been posed. A waiter came by and offered me a menu, which was then abruptly taken away by Pino, who thrust it back at the poor fellow, saying, 'What are you doing? He doesn't need this. I'll make him whatever he wants.' Pino's special treatment of me suddenly put me in mind of Romano's special treatment of my dear long-lost friend Marcello Mastroianni all those years ago. Except Marcello was a cinematic icon with nice hair, and I am not and have none.

As I watched the young waiter recede with embarrassment simply for doing his job well, Pino smiled at me.

'He's a good kid.'

I shook my head and laughed at what I recognized as true Calabrese parenting behaviour. Pino is a very generous man and a kind boss to the many employees who stay with him for years and years, but he can be, shall we say, very straightforward. He admits this himself. He studied medicine for three years before turning to the kitchen, and I believe he would have been an equally brilliant doctor as he is a chef. Still, my instinct is that his bedside manner might have needed a little help.

'So, what would you like?' he asked.

'Just, maybe some pasta. Something simple.'

'With meat? No meat?'

'With meat.'

'Okay.'

And he was off.

Celestino came by and chatted with me for a bit as we had a glass of wine together. As always he asked about my parents and the children and told me how he wanted some day to meet Felicity and the little ones. A few minutes later a bowl of pasta with a Bolognese sauce was placed before me. Celestino was up in a flash.

'Go ahead. I'll let you eat. I'll be back.'

And he was gone. I took a mouthful but was confused as to what it was I tasted. It was a Bolognese sauce, but it had a depth of flavour that I had never experienced before. I ate bite after bite but I couldn't figure it out. I craned my neck looking for Celestino or Pino, but they must have been in the other room. Then Celestino suddenly appeared.

'You okay?'

'Yes, great. What is this?'

'Bolognese,' he said, looking at me like I was a moron.

'No. I know. But why is it . . . ?'

'What?'

'I don't know. Why does it taste like this?'

'You don't like it?'

'No, no. I love it! I just . . . I've never tasted one like this.'

'Pino!' he shouted into the other room.

Silence. Celestino left. I heard him yell Pino's name again from the other room. I ate some more. Pino arrived.

'What's the matter? Something wrong?' he said, and then smiled slyly.

'What the . . . How do you make this?'

'It's good, right?'

'That's an understatement.'

'Okay, here's what I do. I make a stock . . .'

'Yes . . .'

'Of cheese.'

'Wait. What do you mean?'

He explained how he took a piece of Parmigiano rind and made a stock with it by putting it into a muslin bag with some herbs and cooking it in water for an extended period of time. He then used the result to bring an amazing depth of flavour to an already beautiful meat sauce. So simple. Cheese stock. Who knew? Certainly not me.

We chatted for a bit, and realizing I had an early call, I asked him for the check, which he refused to give me. He never lets me pay. He says when I come with friends I can pay, but when I am alone I should think of the restaurant as my home. As we parted and I thanked both brothers effusively, all I could think about was finishing work in good time tomorrow so I might visit my friend Pino, the generous genius, again.

Pino Posteraro's Parmigiano Stock

1 quart water
1 large Parmigiano rind (about 750g)
7 oz coarse sea salt
3 small bay leaves

- Fill a large pot with the water. Wrap the rind in cheesecloth, tie tightly with string, and secure to the side of the pot (this helps avoid the Parmigiano's sinking to the bottom of the pot and burning). Submerge the wrapped rind.

- Add the salt and bay leaves.

- Gently boil for 2 hours, strain, and use for Bolognese.

Pino Posteraro's Fettuccine with Ragout alla Bolognese

– SERVES 4 –

1 tablespoon chopped onions

1 tablespoon chopped carrots

1 tablespoon chopped celery

2 tablespoons extra virgin olive oil

25g mixed fresh herbs (such as rosemary, sage and/or thyme), chopped

2 bay leaves

50g dried porcini mushrooms, reconstituted

225g lean ground beef or veal

25g tomato paste

3½ tablespoons dry white wine

3½ tablespoons freshly squeezed orange juice

1 tablespoon salt

A pinch of black pepper

700ml chicken stock (or Parmigiano stock, page 202)

550ml beef jus (or Parmigiano stock)

300g egg fettuccine

25g butter

25g 36% fat whipping cream (optional)

35g Grana Padano, grated

- In a large saucepan over a medium heat, sweat the vegetables in the olive oil with the herbs and porcini. Add the meat and cook until brown, perhaps utilizing a lid to achieve a better and faster result. Add the tomato paste, wine and orange juice and let the liquids evaporate. Add the salt, pepper and stocks and let simmer for about 1½ hours.

- When the ragout is cooked, boil the fettuccine in salted water until al dente. Add the butter and the cream, if using, to the ragout *alla Bolognese*, toss the pasta with the sauce, and sprinkle with the grated Grana Padano.

14

The Martini

No one really knows the true origins of the drink that E. B. White called 'the elixir of quietude'. Some say a bartender invented it at the end of the 1800s in the town of Martinez, California. Others say other things. Too many people say too many things and I wish they'd stop. In the end it doesn't really matter. The only thing that matters is that the Martini exists. And to me it matters a great deal that it exists in its driest form. (The word 'Martini' will always be capitalized within these pages.)

Originally Martinis were made with a one-to-two ratio of dry vermouth and gin. (If one were using sweet vermouth this would be known as a 'Perfect Martini'.) But over the years Martinis became more and more dry, meaning they used less and less vermouth, to the point where many were made with none at all. Noël Coward suggested that the cocktail of cocktails be made by 'filling a glass with gin and waving it in the general direction of Italy', and I agree. (I have heard that in England during World War II, Scotch was used as a replacement for vermouth, which, for obvious reasons, was hard to come by. This story may well be apocryphal but I like the resourcefulness of the idea, and having often made a Martini this way, I must say it's very tasty.) In my opinion, depending upon the quality and flavour profile of the gin or vodka, little or no vermouth should be used. I also believe that a Martini should be stirred and not shaken, no matter what 007 has told bartenders on screens for the last sixty years. Yet, at Dukes in London, where Mr Fleming supposedly conjured up the ultimate gentleman spy, Martinis are neither shaken nor stirred, unless requested. Frigid potato vodka is poured directly into an ice-cold glass and garnished with one's choice of olives or a lemon twist. Although I pride myself on being able to handle my liquor, due to the absence of ice cubes and their diluting effects on the alcohol, one of these can be enough for me to ask the waiter if he would discreetly remind me of my own name.

I only learned to make a Martini properly not when I was a bartender at Alfredo's many years ago, but when I was a customer many years later. It was in a hotel on Majorca near a house I was staying in while filming a project that barely saw the light of day, thank God. I bellied up to the bar one evening after a rousing game of tennis and ordered a very dry Martini. As usual I watched the bartender like a hawk while he concocted my crepuscular tipple, making sure he had even a vague idea of how to work both shaker and strainer simultaneously. (I have actually been known to talk bartenders through the process very carefully if I see them struggling or ask politely if I can go behind the bar and just make my own.) Luckily, as it turns out, this bartender, who was Italian, more than knew his way around a bar. Here is what he did, and now, thanks to him, this is what I do.

Martini

Ice

Dry vermouth

Gin or vodka

Olives or a lemon twist, to garnish

- Take a glass beaker and fill it with ice.

- Pour in a half shot of good dry vermouth.

- Stir it well for about 15 seconds.

- Let it sit for about 30 seconds.

- Stir it again.

- Strain out the vermouth.

- Pour in 3 to 4 shots of good gin or good vodka.

- Stir it well for about 30 seconds.

- Let it sit for about 30 seconds.

- Stir it again for another 30 seconds.

- Let it sit for another 30 seconds.

- Stir it quickly.

- Strain it into a chilled glass.

- Garnish with either 1 or 3 olives (never 2) or a lemon twist.

- Drink it.

- Become a new person.

I discovered Martinis after graduating college at a restaurant called Café Luxembourg on the Upper West Side of New York. It is an upscale French bistro that has been serving consistently good food for about forty years and I am happy to say is still extant. I didn't have much money at the time, but I would often sit at the polished zinc bar, nurse a Martini or two, and partake of the free hard-boiled eggs that were on offer. A terrible diet, yes, but I was young and this was my right. I was so happy just to be perched at the bar in this kinetic environment reading, writing, or simply observing the well-heeled as they ordered meals and bottles of wine I hoped I could one day afford. At the time Martinis were not nearly as fashionable as they are now, nor were there as many brands of gin or vodka on the market as there are today. But as a hopeless romantic who had a penchant for the 1930s and 40s, I drank them in the hope that they might imbue me with the charm and savoir faire of William Powell or the aforementioned master of caustic wit and wisdom Noël Coward. I normally asked for them to be made with

Bombay gin, which was a stretch for my rather tight budget but well worth it. Then around the mid-eighties, Bombay released their Sapphire brand. Brilliant marketing caused it to become all the rage, and after tasting it once, I immediately 'upgraded' my Martinis despite my meagre earnings. Since my early days at Café Luxembourg, the Martini has been a staple of my diet.

In fact, it is not rare for me to sport a portable Martini kit on a film set, which I put to good use at the end of a day of filming when I have settled back into the makeup chair and the 'mask' is removed, as we actors pompously say. (Well, not *me*, but probably someone like Ryan Reynolds would say that.*) I have used this kit or others like it for many years and it gives me great pleasure to mix a Martini for anyone who craves one at wrap as I do.

During the filming of *Captain America*, the director, Joe Johnston, became so used to them that even if I'd wrapped a bit early, his assistant would knock on the door and ask if I could wait around just a bit longer to make Joe his evening elixir. (I was more than happy to oblige, within reason of course, as he was such a great fellow.) On the same film, Chris Evans, Hayley Atwell and I bonded over Trailer-tinis and we have remained close friends ever since. The wonderful director Barry Sonnenfeld and I always drank a Martini together during our two collaborations on the last shot of every day of filming. For those lucky enough to not be in 'the biz', the last shot of the day is known as

---

* Ryan Reynolds is a very dear friend and would never say such words. But Colin Firth probably would.

'the Martini' and we were simply making sure it lived up to its name. (Speaking of names, I'll pick up all those I've just dropped a little later.)

Over a decade ago, I was lucky enough to work with the brilliant makeup artist Peter King on *The Lovely Bones*. Together we came up with the look of the horrid person I was playing, a rapist/serial killer named Mr Harvey. The director, Peter Jackson, Peter King and I felt it was vital that the character be as unremarkable-looking as possible within the setting of 1970s American suburbia. We achieved this with a wig, false teeth, a fake moustache, blue contact lenses, and a lightening of my skin tone. (Why they didn't hire someone else is still a mystery to me.) With the addition of a false paunch, drab attire and aviator glasses, I was practically unrecognizable and was glad of it as I found the role to be more emotionally and psychologically taxing than any I had ever played. For this reason I could not wait to 'shed' Mr Harvey at the end of every day.

Removing that benign face of evil was freeing indeed, and I must admit, never was a post-wrap Martini more needed. I'd stir up a couple for Peter and myself (luckily he shared my affinity for them and then some), and into the stemmed glass would slip all of the anxiety and emotional discomfort I had felt during that day's filming. Those happy few who have ever experienced a well-made straight-up, dry Martini will know that after the first sip, one is instantly soothed and the world is set right. Of course, any drink at the end of a working day takes the edge off, but a well-made Martini eases and polishes that edge like no other drink I know. And after the second one, that edge is practically bevelled.

In short, whether it is made with gin or with vodka, a Martini is the quintessence of elegance that we all aspire to and believe we acquire when we drink one. However, just as they can elevate a body, they can also be the source of a soul's downfall.

As Dorothy Parker purportedly once said, 'I like to have a Martini, / Two at the very most. / After three, I'm under the table, / After four, I'm under my host.'

15

I met my wife Felicity Blunt at her sister's wedding a little over a year after Kate had died. The wedding took place in Lake Como at a gorgeous home owned by a friend of the affianced couple whose name rhymes with George Clooney. I had taken the train there from Florence as I was staying in Tuscany with my parents, my three children, my stepdaughter, and my father-in-law. This was a trip that Kate and I had always wanted to make with all of the above, but due to her lengthy illness we were never able to, so I had decided to make it in her honour.

The wedding was a three-day affair, and for me, as I had barely been away from my family for some time before Kate's death, it was a welcome and, I discovered, much-needed respite. I saw some dear friends and met a few new ones, including the aforementioned sister of my friend whom I would end up marrying a few years later. Felicity and I chatted over those few days quite a bit, meaning she practically stalked me. (There is CCTV footage.) Most of our discussion centred around food. Conveniently, in about two weeks' time I was to begin filming *Captain America* in London, where she lived, and we decided we would meet up for dinner. Thus began a romance that was . . . food-centric.

During those few weeks in London we ate at many a great restaurant, the first being the recently closed Ledbury, run by two-Michelin-starred chef Brett Graham and above which Felicity conveniently lived.

Now, I am not one who is necessarily drawn to the Michelin star. Often I find that many of the restaurants that have earned this coveted award are a bit fussy, to say the least, and I've left a few of them completely famished, as I have never found pretentiousness very filling. However, this was not the case with the Ledbury.

The small dining room was elegant and the tables quite far apart from one another, and at times it seemed there were more staff than patrons even when it was full. There was a warmth that both the room and the people exuded that put one instantly at ease. I chalk this up to Brett's personality, for as they say, 'The fish stinks from the head down', but in this case it was a good stink. Although the food at the Ledbury was rarefied, Brett himself is not. He is very genial and relaxed for someone who works with such intensity and has maintained a standard of excellence for a very long time. (The Ledbury was voted one of the fifty best restaurants in the world for many years running.)

The first time we ate at the Ledbury, Felicity suggested we order the tasting menu so we might partake of as much of Brett's food as possible and the accompanying wine pairings. Each dish, from the Kumamoto oysters to the stuffed loin of rabbit, was extraordinary. Our subsequent visits inevitably found us ordering the tasting menu almost every time. One night after yet another extraordinary meal, Brett was kind enough to invite us into the kitchen for a tour.

The kitchen was small and unremarkable considering the quality and complexity of the food it brought forth night after night. After a few minutes of perusing, we both noticed two pheasants, quite dead but still intact, feathers and all, lying in a tray on the countertop. We started oohing and ahhing over them and were about to ask Brett how he might prepare them when he asked if we would like to take them home. My wife is an agent and I am an actor, and therefore we both know a good offer when we see one, so, after Brett had explained how to 'cold pluck' them, we spirited the fowl, tray and all, upstairs to her apartment and put them in the fridge overnight.

The next morning was a Saturday, and we awoke with the excitement that comes with knowing one has a passionate mission to complete. We pulled the pheasants out of the fridge, made a morning beverage, and plopped ourselves in front of the television to watch my new favourite show, *Saturday Kitchen*, and pluck our birds. An hour and a half later, our dressing gowns covered in feathers, in the tray lay the denuded carcasses of the avian gifts Brett had bestowed on us the night before. It had been a perfect morning. Two food nerds becoming more emotionally intimate by tearing the feathers from a pair of dead birds. It makes no sense that this would give us both such joy, but in a way, it did. First of all, if you're a food lover, there is always something gratifying about connecting with the veg-etable, the fruit, or whatever animal, whether you've grown it, raised it, or hunted it, before it becomes your food. But to make that con-nection and *then* connect with someone else simultaneously is an exalted, almost spiritual level of foodie intimacy. To me it was one of the most romantic mornings I have ever spent sitting down. I strug-gle to remember how we prepared the pheasant, but in this case, it really doesn't matter. Sometimes the process is more satisfying than the result.

Up until the Ledbury's sudden and very unfortunate closing,* Felicity and I would always go there for dinner on special occasions, and even though Brett was always adding new dishes, if it was on the menu, we'd always order the pheasant as a lovely reminder of when, together, we first plucked.

—————

The second restaurant we would frequent was the now-also-defunct L'Anima, run by chef Francesco Mazzei. (I am actually beginning to wonder if Felicity and I are bad luck.) Like my family, Francesco hails from Calabria, yet his cooking is not focused only on the recipes of that region. Francesco is one of those chefs able to take classic recipes

———

* Like too many restaurants, the Ledbury was forced to close by the COVID-19 pandemic. But the good news is that Brett is the director of a Michelin-starred gastropub in Fulham called the Harwood Arms. However, I've just checked and don't see pheasant on the website menu. I take this as a sign that he probably doesn't want us back.

and breathe new life into them without over-complicating the process or compromising the integrity of the dish. The first time Felicity and I went there our meal lasted a good three hours. There came course after course after delicious course, which we washed down with copious amounts of wine. I finally reached a point where I had to stop eating, not only because my jet lag was kicking in but simply because I was close to bursting.

However, Felicity, dear, slender Felicity, was not ready to stop. She finished her final course as well as the rest of mine and continued chatting away as though it were not close to midnight and she didn't have to be in the office the next morning. Then suddenly, out of the corner of her still-hungry eye, she spotted a cheese cart being rolled through the dining room.

'Oh, a cheese cart! Yum! Let's have some cheese, shall we? Would you like some cheese?'

'Well, I mean . . . sure, if you –'

'Excuse me! Can we please take a peek at the – ???!!!'

She had caught the attention of the waiter with the wheels on wheels and successfully intercepted him even though I am sure he was on his way to another table. (When she wants something, she has the gift of charmingly commanding attention in the way only the British do. Is it the accent? She is not posh, but when she speaks, her education is immediately evident, as are her innate intelligence and warmth. I guess the combination of all these attributes is the reason she is so successful, she has so many lovely friends, and I never win an argument.) Well, anyway, before I knew it the cheese cart was before us and she was interrogating the waiter about the lactic makeup, provenance and flavour profile of each cheese. She then ordered quite a few slabs, which she quickly devoured as though she hadn't eaten in days, along with some dessert wine, compliments of the chef. What happened after that is a blur, but before I knew it we were dating seriously and staving off gout became a part of my daily routine.

Whenever I came to visit Felicity in London, whether with or without my children, we always made it a point to go to L'Anima. Francesco was more and more generous with every visit, oftentimes, in true Italian fashion, refusing payment completely, especially when the kids were with us. We loved his food and the spartan, contemporary design of the space so much that we decided to have our wedding reception there a few years later. Of course we had a series of tastings to figure out what the canapés and various courses would be. (My father-in-law Oliver joined us for one of these gustatory marathons and he still talks about it to this day.) After a few of these ancient-Rome-like ingest fests we decided on a menu that was to feed 156 attendees. When the three-course meal had ended, guests would be encouraged to mingle and casually pluck their way through tables filled with various *dolci* and freely pour from bottles of every digestif available in Great Britain. Francesco suggested that if there were enough wine-soaked stragglers still roistering after midnight, he could serve up '*una spaghettata!*', which is basically a shitload of spaghetti with a simple tomato sauce. We agreed. Thanks to Felicity's meticulous planning, the brilliant staff of L'Anima, and Francesco's culinary prowess, the wedding day was a delicious success.

As I said, we did serve some *dolci* in the form of pastries and the like, but you may notice that I have not mentioned a cake, as in a proper multilevel frosted confection. This is with good reason, as neither Felicity nor I has a sweet tooth, yet we did provide a savoury equivalent. This took the form of a massive six-tiered structure made entirely of . . .

wheels

of

cheese.

On the next page is the wedding menu. Each course is named for one of the three children (Felicity's idea).

29TH SEPTEMBER 2012

WINES
GAVI DI GAVI, MONTEROTONDO, VILLA SPARINA
MAGARI, CA MARCANDA, GAJA
GATTINARA RISERVA

MENU
SMOKED AUBERGINE & BURRATA WITH
ONION JAM AND HAZELNUTS
BEEF TARTARE
SEAFOOD SALAD
PICKLED CUCUMBERS

•

NICOLO'S COURSE
HOME-MADE MALORREDUS WITH CLAMS, COLATURA,
LIGHT TOMATO & BOTTARGA

•

CAMILLA'S COURSE
SALT-CRUSTED LINE-CAUGHT SEA BASS SERVED WITH
EXTRA VIRGIN OLIVE OIL & LEMON DRESSING

•

ISABEL'S COURSE
SPIT-ROAST RIB OF VEAL WITH ROASTED POTATOES
AND ZUCCHINI FRITTI

•

FLOURLESS CHOCOLATE CAKE
FRESH FRUITS
CANNOLI SICILIANI
HOME MADE ICE CREAMS & SORBETS
WEDDING CHEESE CAKE PLATTER
WITH CONDIMENTS AND FRESH FIGS

•

DIGESTIFS IN THE PRIVATE WINE ROOM

PASTA SERVED AT 1 A.M.

16

When Felicity and I were first dating, I was offered a film in the UK, which would require me to be there for four to five months. Because the kids were still young and I couldn't be away from them for that long, they came with me. My parents, who are great company, and also great babysitters, joined us as well. Given the number of people in my entourage, I needed a rather large space. Felicity offered to find a house near her apartment in Notting Hill and help enrol the kids in a small international school for the remainder of the school year. Unfortunately the experience of making the film was a drawn-out, physically exhausting, joyless process only made bearable by a wonderful cast and crew. However, I remember the lengthy stay in a slightly worn town house in London with my family and Felicity, who ended up just moving in with us, as a truly enjoyable one.

The kitchen was in the basement, and though it was hardly up to date, it was workable enough. (Although I did have to buy almost a whole new set of cookware, as what was there seemed to have not been updated, or for that matter cleaned, since before the war that was supposed to end all wars.) Whenever I arrived home from work in good time, we always had dinner together, cooked by my mother, or me when I could sneak my way past her to the stove. One morning, we decided we would prepare a chicken or something of the like that evening for dinner. Felicity said she would roast some potatoes, and as we all love roast potatoes we thought this was a wonderful idea.

That evening as we drank our usual pre-dinner cocktails and snacked on olives, prosciutto, etc., Felicity pulled from a paper bag a load of gorgeous yellow potatoes, peeled them, and placed them in a pot of boiling water. I asked what she was doing and she said, 'I'm making roast potatoes.' I was confused because as far as I have always known, boiling is the opposite of roasting, but I said nothing. A while later I noticed her setting the oven to a very high heat and filling a roasting pan with what seemed like a gallon and a half of goose fat. Again I said nothing. When the potatoes were boiled to her liking, she drained the water, placed the top on the pot, and with oven-mitted hands, grabbed the handles with firm assurance (much in the way a pig farmer grabs the ears of a sow and drags it to slaughter) and shook that pot with a strength and vigour I didn't know her slender frame possessed.

'I'm confused,' I said slowly. 'I thought you were making roasted potatoes.'

'I am,' she said flatly, still rigorously at it.

'So, what's that you're doing right now?'

'I'm fluffing them up.'

'Oh,' said I, now even more confused.

I turned away to get a glass of wine and when I turned back, I saw that Felicity, having completed the fluffing phase, had opened the oven door, from which a plume of oily smoke billowed, and extracted the roasting pan of bubbling goose fat. My parents and I were doing our best not to panic as the room filled with smoke and Felicity gently placed the pan of scalding liquid avian flab on the stovetop.

'Sorry. Bit smoky!' she said, laughing and sounding more British than ever, as we ran to open the windows and disarm the fire alarm.

'What the hell are you doing?' I finally asked.

'I'm making roast potatoes!'

'Like that?'

'Yes!' she said, irritation creeping into her voice.

'But, what's all the oil?' I asked, trying to remain calm.

'It's goose fat. And that's what you roast them in! Just . . . relax.'

I noticed that my father was standing by the open door that led to the garden and was fanning away the smoke with a tea towel, and that my mother was standing in the kitchen doorway safely away from the roiling pan of fat, looking on with furrowed brow. Felicity then calmly took the potatoes, one by one, placed them gently in the pan, and slid the whole thing expertly back into the oven. There was silence for a moment.

'When you said roasted potatoes, I thought that you meant –'

'You thought I meant the way you make them,' she said with a smile.

'Yes. Just cut them up, a little garlic –'

My mother, having crept slowly back into the room, chimed in. 'Yes, with garlic, olive oil, rosemary and salt, and then just . . . you know . . . roasted.'

Felicity smiled and laughed. 'Oh, yes, those. I love those but these are how we do them. English roast potatoes. They're what you have with a Sunday roast. These and Yorkshire puddings. My nana taught my mother and me.'

'That's how much oil they used?' I asked doubtfully.

'Goose fat.'

'Sorry, goose fat.'

'You can use oil if you like –'

'What kind?' asked my now-curious mother, having crept fully back into the room, presuming the coast was clear.

'Vegetable. But goose fat is best. It just gives them a richer flavour. And to answer your question, *dear*,' she said pointedly to me, '*yes*, this *is* the amount of oil they used. These will be delicious, I promise.'

'Well, I hope so, because you almost burned the house down,' I quipped.

There was a second of silence.

Felicity glared at me. As did my parents.

Instantly, like duelling Judas Iscariots, the two people who brought me into this world sided with my lover and turned on me, saying things like, 'She knows what she's doing! It's fine! It's just a little smoke! Leave her alone . . .' etc.

At that moment the oven began to erupt once again. Upon seeing the fatty fumes, my parents immediately retreated to the open doorways for safety but continued to take up cudgels on Felicity's behalf.

'Whoops!' said Felicity with a laugh, grabbing a mitt and a fork. Opening the oven door, she eased out the pan, turned the potatoes gently with a fork, slid them back in again, and closed the door.

'There we are!' she said through more oily plumes. 'Not much longer now!'

I was in love. And so were my parents. And then we ate her potatoes and fell in love again.

Felicity's 'Rule, Britannia!' Roast Potatoes

– SERVES 4 –

1kg russet potatoes, peeled and cut into 5cm pieces
Sea salt
2 to 3 tablespoons vegetable oil or goose fat

- Preheat the oven to 200°C.

- Place the potatoes in a large saucepan with a pinch of salt and add enough water to cover. Bring the water to a boil and parboil the potatoes for about 10 minutes. (Do not overcook them – otherwise you will end up with mush at the next step. The outside needs to be just soft enough to be scored with a fork.) Drain the potatoes and return them to the pan. Put a lid on the pan and shake the hell out of it, breaking up and fluffing the outside of the potato pieces. Set aside.

• Pour the oil or fat into a metal or enamel roasting pan and place it in the oven until it's really hot. Remove the pan from the oven and place it on the stovetop over low heat. Put the potatoes in the oil and turn them in it several times to coat. Then roast them in the oven for a good hour, turning them twice during the cooking time.

Joan and Stan's (Safely) Roasted Potatoes

– SERVES 4 –

10 large Yukon Gold or baking potatoes, peeled and quartered, or red potatoes, unpeeled and quartered
4 garlic cloves, cut in half
1 tablespoon chopped fresh rosemary leaves
2 teaspoons chopped fresh oregano leaves, or ½ teaspoon dried
Sea salt
Freshly ground black pepper
50ml olive oil

- Preheat the oven to 190°C.

- Place the potatoes in a large baking dish or casserole. Add the garlic, rosemary and oregano and season with salt and pepper. Drizzle the olive oil over the potatoes and toss to coat evenly. Bake, stirring occasionally, until the potatoes are browned and cooked through, about 1½ hours. Serve immediately.

17

During one of the first trips Felicity made to visit us in West-chester before we married, she suggested that we throw a party. In fact she suggested we throw a party and cook a suckling pig. I immediately agreed, as I love suckling pig and so do the children. Our invites completed, Felicity and I called the butcher in the next town about acquiring said piglet, and he assured us he'd be able to get one before the weekend. But I must digress here for a moment to discuss something that is slipping away – and it's not one of my discs.

When I was younger, and certainly before I was born, butcher shops and fishmongers were fairly common, until giant supermarkets overwhelmed the suburbs, and now sadly our cities, making them redundant. Those few that still exist today are usually quite good, but for the most part, their selections are not very adventurous and their prices are very dear. This, however, is one of the things I love most about living in England. Although I know individually owned butcher shops and fishmongers are disappearing in the UK as well, there are still a fair number of them compared to the US. I am very lucky to have one of each, both of very high quality, within walking distance of my home, and I visit one or the other every few days. But even when I am out and about running errands or in between meetings in different neighbourhoods of London, I can't help but walk into any butcher shop or fishmonger I come across to simply peruse. I visit them in the same way I visit an art gallery. I'm not necessarily there to buy; I just want to see the exhibit. I love that many butchers in London still wear banded straw hats as in days of olde, and that besides the usual cuts of meat and sausages, all different kinds of offal are on offer, again something rarely seen these days in the States. I know that bloody trays containing severed parts of various animals put many people off, but I am fascinated by them and the myriad ways they can be turned into something delicious.

Most people are also put off by the smells emitted by a fish market or a fishmonger's and will hold their noses as they pass by. But I take a deep breath in and find it impossible not to enter, or at least peer greedily through the window. I love that cutting smell of brine that emanates from a colourful collection of fresh fish. I love the way they are so proudly displayed in the windows and refrigerated cases, the shine and glimmer of their scales enhanced by the bright lights above and the crystals of crushed ice below. I love to watch fishmongers deftly scale and debone a fish as they chat to a customer about how fresh it is, explain that bad weather is the reason for the lack of a certain catch, or at times suggest a method for preparing the sea creature in hand to a customer who is fish fearful.

It still surprises me how many people don't eat fish, but also how many don't really cook it because they are intimidated by it. This is where the fishmonger is vital. Not only will you most likely get a premium product from someone who knows its source, whether it's sustainable, when it came in, and how long it will last in the fridge (all of which I know can be found written on packaged fish these days), but the fishmonger will also be able to impart to you the knowledge of how to cook it even in the most basic way. It is this interaction between customer and purveyor that then makes our connection to whatever it is we are buying stronger. To me, eating well is not just about what tastes good but about the connections that are made through the food itself. I am hardly saying anything new by stating that our links to what we eat have practically disappeared beneath sheets of plastic wrap. But what are also disappearing are the wonderful, vital human connections we're able to make when we buy something we *love to eat* from someone who *loves to sell it*, who bought it from someone who *loves to grow, catch, or raise it*. Whether we know it or not, great comfort is found in these relationships, and they are very much a part of what solidifies a community.

There's a wonderful book called *The Great Good Place* by Ray Oldenburg. In it he writes about how we have two places that are crucial to us, *home* being the first and *work* being the second. But equally crucial, because it allows us to function better in the first two, is what he calls *the third place*. These 'third places' are bars, cafés and restaurants. They bring people from all walks of life together and allow for casual interaction with others *with whom we don't work* and *to whom we are not related.* As we know, particularly after a global pandemic, this interaction is vital for the individual and society as a whole in order for both to function well and flourish. I would argue that independent shops, perhaps especially food shops, also fulfil this objective, for the reasons I've mentioned above, and the loss of them to a tsunami of chain stores is a tragedy for us all.

Walking into my local fishmonger's, I am greeted heartily, asked about the children, chitchatted with about the weather and such, and told what catch they personally think is 'lovely' on any given day. They then ask what dish I'm making. If I say I'm making a seafood stew, the first question is, 'For how many?' and we are off together to choose from their icy displays any combination of cod, hake, haddock, clams, mussels, prawns, langoustines and scallops for said stew, oysters for an appetizer, and samphire simply because I have to buy it if it's available.* As each ingredient is chosen we discuss whether the size or count is sufficient for the number of guests. When everything is weighed, wrapped and bagged, the fishmonger will always throw a whole lemon or two and a few sprigs of curly parsley into the bag as well as a small container of their homemade frozen fish stock. Yes, it has cost a pretty penny, but it is well worth it. We say goodbye knowing that in the coming days we will wave to each other as I walk by their shop and soon conspire about how much of any given fish,

---

* I had never tasted samphire until I came to the UK, and instantly took to its briny sweetness.

crustacean or mollusc will be needed when I am again lucky enough to grace my table with their aquatic gems.

But I was writing about a pig.

So Felicity and I drove to the butcher shop in nearby Ridgefield, Connecticut, on a Friday afternoon; bought the suckling pig, which weighed about twenty pounds; and brought it home. It was our intention to put it on the rotisserie on the outdoor barbecue because it was too big to fit in our ovens; however, the pig ended up being too long even for the rotisserie. I did have a wood-burning pizza oven in which it would fit, but having never attempted to cook a suckling pig before, and worrying about my inability to keep the oven at a consistent temperature, I decided that would surely lead to disaster. We had but one choice: decapitation. I grabbed a large carbon steel knife and a cleaver, both of which had belonged to my paternal grandfather, to carry out the act. He had used them for the skinning and breaking down of deer he'd shot on hunting trips to Vermont, where he owned property. So, channelling the first Stanley Tucci, I cut the flesh away from the neck with the knife and dealt the severing final blows with the cleaver and lessened the length of our porcine purchase. We then impaled it with the spit and brought it over to the barbecue, and it was a perfect fit.

At that very moment, the school bus deposited all three children at the end of the drive, and across the lawn they came a-runnin' with the added burst of giddy energy that all kids have on Friday afternoons.

'Hey, guys, come and see what we got!' I shouted.

'Is it the PIG??!!!' they screamed.

'Yes!'

They scurried up the patio steps, hurled their backpacks to the ground, and looked at the pig quizzically.

'Where's the head?' they asked.

'We had to cut it off because it didn't fit on the barbecue.'

'Awwwww,' they moaned. 'Why didn't you wait for us!?'

Felicity and I looked at each other.

'Sorry,' I said. 'I didn't think –'

'We'll get another pig some day and then you can watch us cut its head off,' said Felicity ever so sweetly, sounding like a Hollywood serial killer.

They were not convinced.

'Where is it?' they asked.

'Right here,' I said, taking it down from the counter for them to ogle.

'Wow!'

They began to poke and prod it with their little digits, examining its mouth and eyes like frustrated, clumsy veterinarians.

'What're you gonna do with it?'

'Well, I was actually going to just try slow-roasting it in the pizza oven.'

'Ohhhhh, yeah. Wow . . .' they said, as though they were going to eat it, which I knew they wouldn't. They only craved the soft juicy white meat of the carcass and the crunch of the cracklings.

After they spent a bit more time looking at the head and

making pre-adolescent comments about the fact that the rotisserie spit is shoved unkindly up the pig's rectum, we shooed them inside to wash their hands and made the opposite of slow-roasted pig's head, their usual afternoon snack of Ritz crackers slathered with peanut butter.

The next day we cooked the pig as planned, but unfortunately it was too heavy for the rotisserie, which ended up breaking halfway through. My friend Oliver Platt – a great foodie – and I took turns spinning the thing by hand every few minutes. Needless to say the pig was not a great success, and neither was my attempt at slow-roasting the head. Consumed with the task of overseeing the carcass, I neglected the head completely, only remembering it later that afternoon. Opening the pizza oven, I was confronted with a sight from a horror film that I won't describe here. Suffice it to say, I don't like horror films.

The second time we tried to cook a whole pig – the pig redux – we were lucky enough to have a professional on hand to help us, by the name of Adam Perry Lang. Adam is a chef and restaurateur who can cook anything brilliantly but whose primary passion and expertise is meat. He was co-owner of a restaurant with Jamie Oliver called Barbecoa in London, connected to a butcher shop that sold some of the best beef, fowl and game in the city. (Sadly both are now defunct.) Adam left London seven years ago to return to the US and now owns APL in Los Angeles with his friend the food fanatic and all-around mensch Jimmy Kimmel. It was these two fellows and their wives who sent Felicity and me a Caja China as an engagement present. I had no idea what a Caja China was, although once confronted with it I realized I had indeed seen one before.

A Caja China is basically a rectangular metal box set into an aluminium and plywood frame on wheels. The box is large enough to fit a side of beef, a huge amount of ribs, or probably about twenty chickens. But most important, an enormous pig. Adam and his then wife, Fleur, were visiting family in New York and came up to stay for the weekend. He told us that they wanted to put the Caja China to good use by roasting a whole pig. He gave us a list of ingredients to buy and said he would procure the pig. Say the word 'pig', and Felicity and I hear the word 'party'. So we threw one.

The day before the party, Adam and Fleur arrived, followed soon afterwards by the pig, all seventy pounds of it. Adam and I carried it out to the patio and placed it on a picnic table covered with a vinyl tablecloth. Here, he deftly sliced the tenderloins from the carcass, as they are too delicate and lean to be cooked in this way, and set them aside, and then we headed inside to make the brine.

The Brine of Adam

- In a large container combine:

2 litres water

50g sea salt

2 tablespoons granulated sugar

2 lemons, cut in half

3 bay leaves, preferably fresh

8 garlic cloves, crushed and peeled

2 tablespoons fresh thyme leaves

1 tablespoon black peppercorns

1 teaspoon red pepper flakes

Once the brine was made, Adam took out a comically large syringe, filled it with the brine, and began the painstaking process of injecting the carcass wherever bone met flesh. This took a while but he assured me it was worth it. We stuffed the animal into a huge plastic cooler bought specifically for this occasion; weighed down the top with heavy rocks to deter any marauding raccoons, of which there were many; and headed inside for drinks and dinner. I remember sipping glasses of a new liquor that Adam had just brought to market, called Moonshine, which was a refined version of, well . . . moonshine. And that's about all I remember of that night.

The next morning we wheeled the Caja China on to the patio, and as it was beginning to rain, I drove to the hardware store to buy a pop-up shelter to shield the coals, which would sit exposed in the tray on top of the pig, cooking it from the top down. The shelter would also cover the paella I planned on making on my outdoor paella maker. In Westchester then, and now in London, there are two outdoor cooking options that I've convinced myself I can't live without. One is a pizza oven and the other is a paella maker, because I adore pizza and I'm in love with paella. The pizza oven is self-explanatory, but the paella maker consists of a huge iron pan that rests atop a round stand in which sit two perforated rings that are connected to a propane gas tank. Making paella outdoors, particularly on this contraption, for guests is one of my greatest joys. It takes a long time and can be a bit tricky, but in the end, no matter what the result, it is worth it if only for the conversation it engenders. The great thing about this Spanish contrivance is that, if one has the time and inclination, one can dispense with the rings of flame and make a wood fire in the stand, place the pan on top, and cook away. Ultimately this is the way it should be made, because the smoke from the fire works its way into the paella, bringing to it new depth. The best paella I've ever made was in a roasting pan over a small outdoor fireplace at my in-laws' house in Portugal, proving that I don't really need to be outfitted with my favourite piece of cooking kit, but I prefer to believe it had more to do with the seafood, wood and ocean breezes of the Algarve than the roasting pan.

I returned from the hardware store to find Adam and my son Nicolo tying long branches of rosemary, thyme and parsley on to the end of a broken broom handle. Adam planned to use this to baste the beast. We left Nicolo to finish the rustic baster while Adam and I erected the pop-up shelter, which ruined the aesthetics of the whole patio for me. I like my surroundings, even at a pig roast, to have a suggestion of elegance, and blue nylon pop-up shelters suggest anything but. However, I let it go. This time. We secured the pig tightly between two racks provided with the Caja China, hauled it into the box, put the top on, scattered the coals, and lit it up. It would now cook from the top down for about four hours. This method of cooking ensures that not only will the meat be incredibly moist and its fat almost melted throughout, but a crusty 'crackling' will be created. This method of cooking is ancient but the invention of the box is recent.

A Cuban immigrant to Florida remembered pig being cooked in a box in this manner by descendants of Chinese immigrants in Cuba, and he and his son built a prototype in 1985. Having achieved the desired result as described above when cooking the pig, they began to manufacture them and still have a very successful business to this day. I had to abandon my Caja China in the US when I moved to London, but I am tempted to buy another, because the pork that emerged from that odd, hot box was extraordinary. However, given the lack of storage space in my house, I may just have to employ it as a cot for our youngest when it's not in use.

Anyway, once the pig was in, I set up the paella maker, Adam returned to the kitchen to prepare the largest batch of chimichurri sauce ever made on the New York–Connecticut border, Fee and Fleur set the table, and the kids shucked acres of corn. Were it not for the cheap and tawdry nylon pop-up shelter, I would have been in heaven.

The Chimichurri of Perry Lang

— MAKES ENOUGH FOR ONE 500G PIECE OF MEAT —
(FOR MORE, INCREASE THE QUANTITIES OF THE
INGREDIENTS ACCORDINGLY)

2 garlic cloves

1 jalapeño (or spicier pepper; optional)

10 sprigs oregano

10 sprigs parsley

2 tablespoons red wine vinegar

3 tablespoons olive oil

½ teaspoon salt

¼ teaspoon black pepper

- Peel the garlic cloves. Smash on a cutting board with the broad side of a chef's knife. Mince.

- Top and deseed the jalapeño pepper, if using. Dice on the same cutting board.

- Pick the oregano and parsley leaves off the sprigs. Pile directly on top of the garlic and roughly chop.

- Add the red wine vinegar, olive oil, salt, and pepper directly on to the board. Mix all.

A few hours later, guests arrived, and when Adam gave me the go-ahead, I began to cook the paella. Some of the teens helped me embed the chicken wings into the rice, and after they'd cooked for a bit we distributed the clams, mussels and shrimp evenly around the pan. For some reason every time I make paella I find that if there is a teenager around they particularly like to help with this part of the cooking process. I don't know why but I'm glad of it. As I said earlier, paella cooked outdoors draws people into its orbit like crows or monkeys are drawn to shiny objects. They linger around the pan as it burbles away, slowly chatting about this and that but all the while taking in the slow transformation that happens as the rice expands and grows deeper in colour as the soffritto works its way into each grain, the molluscs open slowly, and the shrimp change from an opaque blue-white to reddish pink. So many slow-cooked meals are secreted away inside an oven and presented in their finished state, but paella invites one into the process. It has nothing to hide.

With the paella completed, the top of the Caja China was removed, revealing something that looked nothing like the hog that had been placed inside hours before. What we carefully raised from the box was a golden, sumptuous, crackling-encrusted pig that elicited moans and applause from the now-ravenous guests. We laid it on to a table covered with a hodgepodge of cutting boards, released the pig from its racks, and Adam began the process of freeing the meat from its bones as the corn was placed into pots of boiling water to cook for five to ten minutes.

We served it all up on countless paper plates, poured more wine and beer, and raised a glass to the Spanish and Cuban visionaries who had created two of the best dishes ever cooked in an iron pan and a metal box.

———

I got carried away by the pigs. I need to write a little more about fish.

18

Felicity and I both love seafood, and seafood stew is something we cook quite often. It's quick to make; it's healthy; it can be served with pasta, rice or toasted bread to create a complete meal; and it's bloody delicious. As a kid I was never that keen on fish and therefore I never fully appreciated how well my mother, also a seafood lover, cooked anything that came from the water. Many of her specialties were served on Christmas Eve, as I described earlier, but I don't really remember her making a seafood stew. As I began to travel for work and started eating in restaurants more often, I became fascinated by seafood stew and would order it if it was on the menu in any restaurant I went to.

One of my first jobs away from home for an extended period of time was in 1988 in Vancouver, British Columbia. Vancouver was about a quarter of the size it is now, but even then it had some fairly good restaurants. (Now it has some amazing restaurants.) One was a place called Joe Fortes, a sort of old-fashioned seafood and chop house, which is still around. Here they served a fish stew called cioppino. It is said that cioppino was created by Italian fishermen who had immigrated to San Francisco in the early part of the twentieth century and was based on a stew they had made back in Liguria called *ciopin*. Like most fish stews, it is composed of whatever fish were hauled up in the daily catch. I had never heard of it before going to Vancouver but I was very happy to have found it.

There are many versions of fish stew, or in Italian, *zuppa di pesce*, throughout Italy itself and the world over. For instance, in Livorno there is *cacciucco*, in Croatia there is *brudet*, yet another from Liguria is called *burrida*, and of course from Provence there is the brilliant bouillabaisse. (The latter may be my favourite, heretical as that is given my heritage.)

Basically most fish stew recipes are quite similar. However, there are some ingredients that in most places would be acceptable but in certain regions of Italy are blasphemous to use. For instance, I was once explaining to a Tuscan how I made my fish stew, and when I mentioned the word 'onion' she became practically apoplectic.

'No! Never! Onion?'

'Yes, a little –'

'No. Never!' she repeated. 'Never onion with fish!'

'Really?' I asked meekly.

'Yes. Never.'

'Huh, I always find it gives a sweetness –' I ventured, but was abruptly cut off by her saying, 'No. Horrible. Never.'

We stopped talking about seafood stew at that point. As I have said, Italians can be very dogmatic when it comes to food in general.

For the most part seafood stews were created by fishermen to make use of the less marketable bits of their catch or any good bits that went unsold. Often if they were out at sea for long periods they would bring canned or sometimes fresh tomato, garlic, onions, oil and salt with them on board and make stew on the boat with the spoils of the day. The wonderful thing about any fish stew is that you can use inexpensive bits of fish and still make something quite delicious. Of course, more expensive seafood, such as langoustines, lobsters, crabs or tiger prawns, in combination with various pieces of what are now pricier fish, like cod or sea bass, can also be used. Unfortunately most seafood is rather pricey these days, so seafood stew is no longer a poor man's dish, especially if you are making it for a large dinner party. But be that as it may, if you can't find affordable seafood (hit the fishmonger's at the end of the day, as they sometimes give you a discount on bits and pieces of this or that fish that are to be discarded and are perfect for a stew), or if you have a hankering for something richer, then splurge on the best fish, crustaceans and molluscs you can find and have at it.

Here is our recipe for fish stew:

Fish Stew

— SERVES 6 —

1kg fresh mussels (the smaller the better)

1kg fresh vongole *(small clams)*

50g sea salt or cornmeal

1 teaspoon saffron threads (optional)

500ml warm or room-temperature shrimp stock (optional, but it gives a richer flavour)

500ml warm or room-temperature fish stock (if using shrimp stock; if not using shrimp stock as well, have 1 litre ready)

Extra virgin olive oil

4 garlic cloves, cut in half

1 medium onion, diced

650g chopped fresh tomatoes

3 basil leaves, torn in half

Sea salt

2 whole pepperoncini (optional)

500ml white wine

Freshly ground black pepper

12 medium shrimp, shells on

500g fresh cod (or similar fish), cut into small chunks

500g fresh monkfish (or similar fish), cut into small chunks

A handful of fresh parsley, chopped

Good toasted bread, for serving

- Wash and pull the 'beards' off the mussels.

- Place the *vongole* and mussels in separate bowls of cold water, add the salt or cornmeal, and leave to purge for about an hour.

- After the mussels and *vongole* have purged, place half of each into a large frying pan of boiling salted water and cover for a few minutes until they have opened. Then remove the meat from the shells, place it in a bowl, and set aside. Discard the shells.

- Sprinkle the saffron threads, if using, into a cupful of the stock and let dissolve.

- In a medium sauté pan drizzle a glug of the olive oil and add 1 garlic clove and half of the chopped onion. Simmer on a low to medium heat until soft, about 5 minutes. Add the chopped tomatoes, basil and a large pinch of salt. Cook down until the tomatoes have softened and the mixture begins to gel. About 10 minutes.

- In a large, deep frying pan or a pot, pour in a glug of olive oil and sauté the rest of the onion and garlic over a medium-low heat until softened and clear. If using pepperoncini, they can be sautéd now as well.

- Add the white wine to the pan and raise the heat to allow the alcohol to evaporate.

- Reduce the heat to medium and add the fresh tomato sauce as well as the stock, including the saffron-infused stock. Add salt and pepper to taste. Let cook for a few minutes.

- The sauce should now be at a slow boil. Add the clams and mussels that are still in their shells and cover. After 2 minutes, add the shrimp and cover. After 2 more minutes, add the fish and the reserved clam and mussel meat. Cover and cook for about 2 minutes. Turn off the heat and move the lid so it is slightly askew. Add a drizzle of extra virgin olive oil. Taste and add more salt or pepper if needed. Let rest for about 10 minutes.

- Ladle into large bowls, sprinkling each with chopped parsley and a drizzle of olive oil. Serve with the toasted bread.

———

I said that Felicity and I love seafood. We also love the sea, particularly the Amalfi coast, so when friends invited us to join them for a few days on a private yacht a wealthy friend had loaned them, we jumped at the chance. I find dining al fresco on a beautiful day, no matter what the season, one of the most enjoyable experiences ever. Dining al fresco at a restaurant in any part of Italy is even *more* enjoyable. Sailing on a *yacht* and dining al fresco on the Amalfi coast is *so enjoyable* that one feels guilty. (Well, I do.) The fresh salty sea air and sunshine augment whatever is on one's plate or in one's glass. The ease of summer life there, and the generosity of the Amalfitani, can't help but strip away all worries and open even the most stubborn of hearts.

Travelling with Felicity is always a pleasure. She is incredibly organized and well researched, particularly when it comes to restaurants. She also knows how to use 'apps' and things on mobile phones that completely confound me. She taps an icon on her mobile device and something positive happens. Directions are displayed and restaurants are located, hotels are rediscovered, tiny shops hidden away reveal themselves, and food markets emerge miraculously as if from nowhere. When I tap an icon on my phone, often *nothing* happens. This is common, particularly on a cold day, because I have such poor circulation in my fingers that the necessary warmth of a living person needed to activate the device is non-existent in my digits, so, for just a moment or two, I know what it probably feels like to be dead. However, even when I *am* able to open an app, I usually don't know how to use it, so I end up just muttering a few '*Goddamn it!*'s or '*Stupid fucking app piece of shit*', before shoving the device back in my pocket and striding forward, saying something like, 'I think it's this way!' or 'It was here *yesterday!*'

Felicity usually responds with something subtly cynical, like, 'I don't think they moved the Pitti Palace while we slept last night, dear.'

'*Colonialist*,' I whisper darkly as I forge ahead into the void.

But I digress.

Felicity swiftly organized our flights to Italy, asked our hosts where we'd generally be sailing, and began a thorough online search of great restaurants in the vicinity. We flew into Naples and made our way to a marina where our friends were waiting with a small dinghy to take us to the yacht. Needless to say, we were both giddy with excitement. Now, even though I don't swim and get seasick if a boat isn't moving, I actually love boats and I love the sea. I also don't like heights but have no problem going on a chairlift or Alpine gondola, because my passion for skiing eclipses my acrophobia. (I know what you're thinking: *My God, what a fascinating conundrum of a man is that Stanley Tucci.* Whereas my wife is thinking, *My God, how many neuroses can one man have? I wonder if there's an app that can help him?* Termagant.)

Over the next few days we sailed or motored around the coast, either dining on the yacht or stopping off to eat lunch or dinner in Capri or Positano, both of which I have been lucky enough to visit a number of times. One afternoon we headed southward along the coast for lunch at one of Felicity's picks, a much-loved family-run restaurant named Lo Scoglio. Lo Scoglio translates as 'the Rock' or 'the Boulder', but in Italian it refers only to large rocks or boulders by the shore, and the place is aptly named as it juts out of the shoreline and rests on a huge natural stone jetty.

The restaurant is accessible from land by car via the Amalfi Drive or perhaps more romantically by boat, as it is situated right on the beach and the dining area is suspended over the water with a small dock at the end. A portion of this covered dining area can be enclosed by sliding glass windows if the elements should attempt to disturb one's meal, but otherwise it remains open to the sea breezes. It's elegant but not fussy, with that breezy, relaxed air achieved so effortlessly by Italian and French seaside restaurants. The menu is very straightforward, offering *frutti di mare*, whole fresh fish of the day, *pasta alle vongole*, and much of the usual Mediterranean fare. But I noticed something that I had never seen before, a dish called *spaghetti con zucchine alla Nerano*. I inquired about it, and Antonia, one of the owners, who manages the restaurant, told me that it was a specialty of the restaurant and that area in general. She told me it was just *zucchine*, basil, oil and grated cheese. Intrigued, I ordered it.

When the dish arrived I saw that it was exactly as described, spaghetti with sautéd small *zucchine* and basil. But upon tasting it I was unable to reconcile that besides the pasta there were only three other ingredients. I asked Antonia if there was any garlic or cream or parsley in the dish, and she said there wasn't and left our table to actually do her job instead of being interrogated by an unnecessarily suspicious customer. But as I took another mouthful, again I thought that the flavours were too complex for the dish to be made with so few ingredients, and I began to doubt Antonia's insistence that what she had told me was true. When she returned to the table, albeit more hesitantly this time, I asked basically the same questions I had asked her before, but this time around, in Italian. For some reason I thought I might get the truth out of her if she spoke her native language.

'*Non c'e' aglio?*

'*No.*'

'*Da vero?*'

'*Si.*'

'*Un po di crema?*'

'*Certamente, no! Mai.*'

'Prezzemolo?'

'No.'

'Solo, zucchine –'

'Zucchine, basilico, olio, e formaggio.'

'Incredibile.'

Then, in English, I posed the famous question that Peggy Lee asked in song so many years ago: 'Is that all there is?'

Antonia looked at me, smiled wryly, and said, 'Yes, that's all there is.'

I would have made a terrible cop.

Lo Scoglio was founded in 1952 by Antonia's grandparents Peppone and Antoinetta, and now she and her two siblings are the owners of this rather famous establishment that is today also a small fourteen-room hotel. She explained to me that *spaghetti con zucchine alla Nerano* is a very old recipe and by all accounts is what fishermen's wives would cook for their families when *zucchine* were in season. Today this recipe, like so many Italian peasant dishes, is considered a luxury for which anyone will happily pay a pretty penny in restaurants all over the world. (*Cacio e pepe* is another prime example.) I told Antonia, who was warming up to me by now (thank God), yet again how much I loved the dish and asked if she wouldn't mind talking me through its preparation. (Okay, truth be told I had to see the process for myself because I *still* didn't believe there wasn't more to it, and yes, *yes*, to this day, I am still ashamed of doubting this more-than-honourable woman.)

The kitchen at Lo Scoglio is sizeable and needs to be in order to turn out the volume of extraordinary meals they cook on any given day. As we entered, a chef was indeed cooking the *zucchine*. Antonia explained to me that the smaller the *zucchine*, the better, and that a significant number of them must be used in every dish. (If you have ever cooked *zucchine*, you will know that the larger they are, the more water they contain and the less flavoursome they are.) Many recipes for *spaghetti con zucchine alla Nerano* will use garlic as well, or even just flavour the oil with garlic with which the pasta is tossed. But at Lo Scoglio, as Antonia said, no garlic is used at all. (My guilt for not believing her is still palpable as I write this.) The *zucchine* are fried in a large amount of sunflower oil, which causes them to actually soak up less of the oil than if they were cooked in less oil, if that makes any sense (meaning both my sentence and the concept). They are then left to drain on paper towels, salted, and tossed gently with chopped fresh basil. When the pasta is ready, the *zucchine* are put into a pan with olive oil and tossed together with the pasta, basil, some of the pasta water, salt, pepper and Parmigiano. (I have read that provolone del Monaco cheese can also be used, but I have never tried it this way, though hopefully, if I ever finish writing this book, I will.) Antonia told me that they also make the *zucchine* in big batches, add chopped basil and salt, and store it in the fridge overnight, allowing the flavours to amalgamate. The next day the mixture is brought to room temperature and used as needed.

Having ocular evidence that her words were true, I thanked Antonia for her hospitality and vowed I would return, a prospect that I am sure caused her some concern. And as a matter of fact (lucky woman), I am returning to Lo Scoglio in two months' time. It is my intention to stay in one of their rooms, eat *spaghetti con zucchine alla Nerano* for breakfast, lunch and dinner, and not once raise a dubious eyebrow or question a single word spoken by the establishment's noble proprietress.*

Following is the recipe for *spaghetti con zucchine alla Nerano*. Since we introduced it to the kids, immediately upon our return from that trip to the Amalfi coast, it has become one of their favourites. It's also a wonderful dish to make for a family with different dietary desires because it is completely vegetarian but its depth of flavour will surprise and satisfy most carnivores. Although the process of cooking a huge amount of *zucchine* can be a bit slow going, it's worth it. Actually, it's best to make even more *zucchine* than the recipe calls for the night before and store it in the fridge. This makes the task of putting the dish together the next day a very easy one and allows you to have extra *zucchine* to use in the coming days, either in a frittata, as an addition to rice or polenta, or just as a side dish.

The simple but poignant *spaghetti con zucchine alla Nerano*, born from a quartet of oil, basil, cheese and humble squash, points once again to the Italian ability to discover riches where others might find very little.

---

* I have just recently returned from Lo Scoglio and watched Antonia's brother Tomasso make this dish. On the table were all the ingredients as I described above, plus . . . one other. A small dollop of butter! I KNEW IT! PS: Antonia and I still remain friendly, but I wouldn't trust her as far as I could throw her. I'm kidding. I would do anything for her and her family. Always and ever.

Spaghetti con Zucchine alla Nerano

— SERVES 4 —

About 16fl oz sunflower oil or vegetable oil, or, if you choose, olive oil
8 to 10 small zucchine *(courgettes)*
75g chopped fresh basil
Sea salt to taste
Extra virgin olive oil
500g spaghetti
200g grated Parmigiano-Reggiano

- Put the sunflower oil in a large pot and bring to a low boil over medium-high heat.

- Slice the *zucchine* into thin rounds and fry in the oil until they are golden brown. Remove and set aside on paper towels.

- Sprinkle with basil and salt.

- Transfer to a bowl and drizzle liberally with olive oil.

- Boil the pasta until al dente and strain, reserving about two cupfuls of the pasta water.

- Place the cooked pasta in a large pan or pot over low heat along with the *zucchine* mixture and combine gently. Add the pasta water, a little at a time, to create a creamy texture. You may not use all of the pasta water. Now add some of the Parmigiano to the mixture and continue to combine by stirring gently and tossing. When the mixture has a slight creaminess, remove from the stove and serve immediately.

Note: The *zucchine* mixture can be refrigerated for about 5 days for use at a later date. Best to bring it to room temperature before using.

19

The sense of freedom that sailing the Amalfi coast engendered is in stark juxtaposition to the restrictive lifestyle that March 2020 brought upon us all, also known as the first lockdown. (The one that we thought was going to be the *only* lockdown.) I wrote this piece during that time. It chronicles a day in our lives and the events of that day, which then just basically repeated themselves for months.

We were in London: my wife, Felicity, and I were sequestered there with our two small children, a boy, five, and a girl, two; my three older children, a girl, eighteen, and boy/girl twins, twenty; and a girlfriend of theirs from university who was unable to get to her parents overseas.

Cramming all of these people with differing personalities, ages, needs, wants, etc. in a house for six weeks created an interesting dynamic. For the most part things went very well, meaning no one murdered anyone.

At first I had grand plans for what we might do to pass the time in convivial and entertaining ways. I thought perhaps a rotating schedule of cooks for the nightly meal, followed by movies, games, or Bordeaux-fuelled charades by the fire. Things didn't quite work out that way. Instead, here's what our typical lockdown day looked like with the absence of our nanny and our weekly cleaning lady.

7:00 a.m. GMT

Within moments of Felicity's and my awakening, our five-year-old is in our room. It's not clear how he knows we're awake. For all we know, he has a monitor like the one we use to listen to his two-year-old sister. He waltzes over to my wife's side of the bed, completely ignoring me as usual, and begins to chat with her about nothing and everything. (His usual topic is dragons, as he is obsessed with the wonderful book series *How to Train Your Dragon* and its various cinematic spin-offs.) Felicity and I head to the bathroom and he follows, and perches himself on the bidet to regale us with plot points from the novels and observations about the seemingly endless variety of dragons and their specific attributes. He will carry on this way more or less until sunset.

After dressing, we head to his sister's room, where she has been 'singing' in her crib and perusing the shredded remains of her extensive Peppa Pig book collection. When she sees us enter she inevitably covers her face with a book and pretends to be asleep. She thinks this is funny. She is right. I change her nappy and she kicks me in the groin a few times for my trouble.

We all head downstairs for breakfast. For me, this consists of a double espresso, orange juice, and a bowl of cereal with a banana and almond milk. I also choke down a handful of vitamins, including D_3, K_2, C, B_{12}, curcumin powder and joint supplements, so my knees don't crack like a melting glacier every time I bend down to pick up a rogue Lego block. Felicity has her tea and the children have either toast, cereal, fruit, the occasional egg, or whatever else their little hearts desire. Most of their food ends up on the floor anyway. This precipitates my first deep-clean of the day.

8:00 a.m. GMT

I tidy up their mess, empty the dishwashers – yes, we have two – scour the counters, wipe down the cabinets and their handles, and organize the contents of the fridge, discarding anything past its due date. I also sweep the floor, but after summoning considerable will-power, I decide to delay the mopping for after lunch.

As you might have gleaned, I am a very tidy person. I actually like to clean, as I find it soothing. But I have gone a bit above and beyond during lockdown. The other day, it occurred to me that I might be able to strap a vacuum to my back like a leaf blower so that it could be with me at all times. Not a good sign.

8:45 a.m. GMT

Felicity and I do an online workout with a friend of ours who is a Pilates teacher. The night before we asked one of the older children to come down this morning and babysit. Seconds before the class begins, the bleary-eyed designee emerges, face still swollen from sleep, and grunts a 'Good morning' as we flee to the living room for a fitness-filled escape from reality. During this time I think about what we might cook that evening for eight people yet again.

9:45 a.m. GMT

When the session ends, Felicity and I go over what food items need to be restocked. With four people between the ages of eighteen and twenty, the amount of food, beer and wine that is consumed is staggering. If there is a shortage of avocados at the local stores, it's because we've eaten them all. If there is no Kerrygold butter left in the UK, it's because either it's in our freezer or we ate it. All of it. Just fucking ate it. Probably without even spreading it on anything. I saw a neighbour hungrily eyeing our cat yesterday and it occurred to me that the woman probably hadn't eaten meat in a week because my gluttonous family devoured all of the beef, lamb, veal, chicken, oxtail, pork, rabbit and game in southwest London. Still gasping for breath from an unnecessarily gruelling workout, I rummage through the fridge.

Given our short supplies, I decide to make something simple tonight: *pasta alla Norma* and sautéd lamb chops. I reckon that these two dishes should satisfy everyone's palate and nutritional needs, although I know that my eighteen-year-old daughter will only eat the pasta dish as she is now a vegetarian. What timing.

Pasta alla Norma

2 large garlic cloves, halved
Extra virgin olive oil
2 large eggplants (aubergines), diced
Sea salt
1 litre marinara sauce
500g pasta (rigatoni, ziti or a thick spaghetti)
A handful of basil, roughly chopped
A handful of grated ricotta salata or Pecorino

- In a very large frying pan, fry the garlic in a glug of oil over a low heat for about 2 minutes. Add the eggplant, raise to a medium heat and cook for about 15 minutes, until slightly golden. Salt to taste.

- Add the marinara sauce and cook for about 5 minutes more.

- Cook the pasta and drain, reserving half a cupful of the water.

- Stir the reserved pasta water into the pan mixture and sprinkle with the basil. Measure about three-quarters of the sauce and put it in a serving bowl. Add the drained pasta to the pan with the remainder of the sauce and gently stir it all together. Sprinkle with grated ricotta salata or Pecorino and serve with the extra sauce on the side.

10:30 a.m. GMT

After doing some home-schooling with the five-year-old, Felicity heads upstairs to shower and begin her remote workday from our bedroom. She is a literary agent and carries out her endless meetings via Zoom. With the exception of finishing voiceover work remotely from my studio for a CNN series I recently completed, I have very little to do these days, as film and TV production have shut down. As far as I know, this has never happened since somebody first called, '*Action!*' over one hundred years ago.

So, I do the laundry; play with the kids, often made-up games like 'Mean King', where I affect a very posh British accent and they come to me to 'pay their taxes' and then 'steal' them back when I 'take a nap'. I like this game because I get to sit on my 'throne', an Eero Saarinen womb chair, the most comfortable seating device ever designed. I try to drag the game out for as long as possible so I don't have to get up, but the two-year-old is beginning to reek and I realize I have been neglectful in my nappy-changing duties.

When this wrestling match has ended and she has accused everyone in the house of pooping besides herself, I change both children out of their pyjamas and into the outfit of the day. Although the five-year-old can dress himself, today he insists he is incapable of doing so. I therefore talk him through each stage while the two-year-old hurtles through the room screaming with laughter and jeering at me. I finally catch her, body-slam her to the sofa, and stuff her into her first of many outfits of the day, like sausage meat into a casing. My glasses are nowhere to be found and therefore I can't see well enough to work the minuscule buttons on children's clothing, so I leave part of her outfit undone, hoping Felicity won't notice. (She doesn't. But I do and it plagues me for the rest of the day.)

11:00 a.m. GMT

Once the children are dressed, I usher them into the garden, where they bounce on the trampoline and beg me to allow them to play with the hose. Sometimes I will bounce or 'wrestle' with them for a bit, and this makes them very happy. It has the same effect on me as well. After a while I finally relent and allow them some water play, with a hose, buckets and a miniature plastic kitchen set.

With the kids sufficiently distracted, I head inside and begin cooking, keeping an eye on them from the kitchen window. I first decide to make chicken stock with leftover carcasses.

Simple Chicken Stock

1 chicken carcass (without meat), and
1 whole chicken without breast meat (or 2 of either one)
10 mixed peppercorns
1 medium yellow onion, skin on, cut in half
1 medium red onion, skin on, cut in half
2 garlic cloves, skin on
2 celery stalks, quartered
2 carrots, quartered

A handful of parsley
2 bay leaves
Salt
1 sprig rosemary
2 sprigs thyme

- Put the carcasses into a stockpot, and cover with water. (If you are using a whole chicken cut it in pieces at the leg joints.) Bring to a boil and skim off the scum that rises to the top. Add the other ingredients and simmer, partially covered, for as long as you want but at least 2 hours.

- Strain through a sieve into some vessel and allow to cool, then refrigerate or divide among freezer bags and freeze.

12:15 p.m. GMT

The older generation of children awakens. They enter the kitchen and make quick work of an entire loaf of bread, two pints of cherry tomatoes, four avocados, six eggs, two pints of blueberries, four bananas, twenty rashers of bacon, one litre of almond milk, six Nespresso pods, and a litre of orange juice before retreating to the TV room or their bedrooms, where they tell me they are doing their schoolwork. I believe them, even if I don't. Felicity comes down and serves the little ones lunch after I have changed their waterlogged clothes. I am off to clean a bathroom or two, do some more laundry, or vacuum something that I just vacuumed three hours before.

1:45 p.m. GMT

Felicity puts the two-year-old down for her nap, the five-year-old listens to his audiobook, and I make marinara and prep the eggplant for the *pasta alla Norma*.

3:00 p.m. GMT

When all is prepped and the kitchen is cleaned once again, it is my intention to write something, read, or catch up on emails. Instead I pick up the *New York Times* crossword puzzle to clear my head, and promptly fall asleep.

3:30 p.m. GMT

I awaken with spittle on my chin and too few clues answered. Glancing at my watch, I rush upstairs to awaken the two-year-old from her nap. When I arrive Felicity is already changing her while doing a conference call. I know she wants to give me a dirty look, but she is a much better person than that. I take the child, finish the diapering, re-dress her, and head downstairs. I give both children a snack and we play together in the garden. We bounce on the trampoline, do chalk drawings on the patio, look for slugs, and maybe do some painting. It is at once lovely and exhausting. We are laughing one moment and the next someone is weeping, and I am adjudicating, saying things like, 'Let her have it for a few minutes and then you can have it.'

'What's a few?'

'A few is three.'

'Three minutes?'

'Yes, three minutes. And then you can have it.'

'Will you time it?'

'Yes, I will time it.'

I do indeed time it, but the two-year-old screams when whatever object they both covet gets taken from her. Play begins anew, but then the spat starts all over again.

4:30 p.m. GMT

I look at my watch and will it to be five p.m. Cocktail time.

4:45 p.m. GMT

I acquiesce and make a Negroni. It is said that Negronis are like breasts: 'One is not enough, two is perfect, and three is just too many.'

Today I am tempted to see what happens if I drink four.

5:00 p.m. GMT

The older children have now come downstairs to eat an entire meal before I make them an entire meal for dinner. Thankfully, as penance, two of them take the little ones up for their bath. Felicity enters the kitchen and begs for a Negroni. I gladly make her one, as I hate to drink alone, although I have been known to make near-daily exceptions. And anyway one is never really drinking alone. Someone else is always drinking somewhere. We prepare the children's dinner, lamb chops, rice and string beans. I switch to white wine and thank Christ it is evening.

Lamb Chops

— SERVES 4 ADULTS —

A glug of extra virgin olive oil
3 garlic cloves, halved
10 to 12 lamb chops, salted an hour before using
White wine
A teaspoon of fresh rosemary
A teaspoon of fresh thyme

- In a large cast-iron pan, splash in a tiny bit of the oil and add the garlic. Cook over low heat for about 3 minutes. Remove and set aside. Raise the heat to medium-high and sear the lamb chops until they are browned, 2 to 3 minutes for each side. You may do this in two batches.

- Remove the chops from the pan and set them aside on a platter. Add a splash of white wine, and perhaps a little water, and deglaze. Return the garlic to the pan along with the herbs. Cook for maybe a minute. Pour over the lamb chops and tent with foil for 5 minutes before serving.

6:00 p.m. GMT

The little ones eat their meal, which at times requires us to coax, plead or threaten, spewing old chestnuts such as, 'There will be no dessert for you, young man,' and 'Do you think dragons leave food on their plates?'

'Dragons don't use plates.'

'I know they don't use plates, I know that. I'm just saying . . . could you please just finish it.'

After their meal is eaten, sort of, the little ones are allowed to watch a bit of television. Dragons for him, Peppa Pig for her. (There is no question that my wife and I, along with many parents, wish the creators of that irritating animated swine a slow death, but they are so rich they have probably purchased immortality. And yet at the same time said pig allows us respite for half an hour or so every day. May God bless those creators.)

While the little kids are immersed, I begin to make culinary preparations for the next 'sitting'.

TV time has ended, and we usher the little ones to bed. As usual the two-year-old is screaming between gulps of her bottle because she has had to leave her beloved pink porcine pal. After settling her into her cot, we then take turns reading about dragons to the five-year-old, who proceeds to tell us he's hungry, so we begrudgingly make him some toast and say something like, 'I told you to eat your dinner. This is the last time.'

And it is. Until tomorrow.

7:45 p.m. GMT

Felicity and I cook dinner for ourselves and the four other human locusts and eat standing around the kitchen island because we can't be bothered to set the table any more. We eat, drink wine, and comment on the food, but this past week we've barely spoken to each other. This makes me sad, as I know it's because we are all lost in our own anxieties. I am sure the twenty-year-olds are thinking about whether their year abroad will happen at all, and my eighteen-year-old is lost in worried wonder as to how universities will decide who gets accepted and who doesn't without anyone's having taken exams. Felicity is worried about her assistant being furloughed, if her parents are staying safe, and a thousand other things. I wonder if my very social parents are *really* practising social distancing and what jobs will be available when this is over, and I know already that I most likely will have to be away for a while working on one of them to fill the coffers.

But no matter how frustrated we all are with the situation, I know we can't help but think how lucky we are to have each other, a roof over our heads, food in our bellies, and no symptoms of illness. Only a couple of miles away in any direction there are hospitals chock-full of ill and dying patients who are being attended to by overworked and overwhelmed National Health Service doctors, nurses and support staff. Other than sending cheques and raising money for charities and the NHS by making videos at home, we are helpless to do anything for fear of infection. As we eat in silence, we are all hoping this will end soon without too much more suffering, that our leaders will get at least one thing right along the way, and that the next time we are all sequestered together, it is by choice.

9:15 p.m. GMT

The kitchen has been cleaned by group effort and we head our separate ways, the kids to the TV room, my wife and I to the sitting room to read. In a short while I'll climb the stairs and head to bed, knees creaking, as I plan tomorrow night's meal. Chicken cutlets for the little kids, mushroom risotto for the rest of us.

———

It is nearly a year since the beginning of the first lockdown and we are now almost six weeks into the second. Obviously the first one didn't work. However, it seems that people are taking things more seriously now, with a few exceptions, sticking to the rules. The vaccines are being rolled out and the number of cases and deaths is shrinking significantly, something for which we are all thankful. During the first few weeks of this lockdown all the kids were home, including Isabel's boyfriend, so lots of food was being bought, cooked and consumed similarly to what is documented above. But now, in order to preserve their sanity, Nicolo has returned to his flat and his 'mates' (as he now calls his friends) in Brighton to continue university online, while Isabel and her boyfriend have retreated to his place. Only poor Camilla is stuck with me and Felicity, Matteo and Emilia. Yet, unlike during lockdown number one, Emilia is now speaking in full sentences (although some are often completely incomprehensible) and talks almost as incessantly as her brother. Fun for all. (Actually it is.)

To look after her mental health, Camilla has bought a sewing machine and retreats to her room often to 'thread her bobbins', she says. However, I can't help but think that she's probably stitching together a hot-air balloon in which to sail away from us all. Can't say I blame her. I did notice that some bedsheets were missing and all our Fortnum & Mason hampers have vanished. Hmmm.

As for Felicity and myself, we only have five people to cook for this time around.

Gosh, it's almost too easy.

Almost.

20

I find being in Los Angeles for any longer than a few days rather painful. I have felt that way about the place since my first visit about thirty-four years ago. Although there are lovely areas, some wonderful restaurants, and close friends and family members whom I love dearly, it just ain't for me. I don't care for the consistent sunshine, the lack of rain, the absence of seasons, and the sprawl of it all.

Four years ago I found myself there after an absence of more than five years, filming a limited series called *Feud*. I flew back and forth a number of times from LA to London, so as not to be away for too long at any one time, but often had to stay longer than I had hoped due to the schedule. The pain of being away from my family was, of course, palpable, but more palpable was a shooting pain in my jaw. This pain had been coming and going for a while, but when I was in LA it worsened. I found a wonderful dentist who couldn't quite discern what was wrong but told me to come back and check with her if it persisted. I flew back to London and had a wisdom tooth removed at the request of my dentist there, as we both thought that it was too close to the adjacent tooth and food was getting trapped in between and causing the issue. (I know that's a gross image in any book, let alone a food memoir, and I apologize.) Yet after the removal the pain got worse. Back in LA, I returned to the first dentist, who examined me and suggested that it might be a form of oral cancer.

I was stunned to the point of almost fainting. Kate had died after a horrid four-year struggle with cancer and the thought of revisiting that world again was something I dreaded. The dentist suggested I get a scan right away. I was leaving that evening and decided I would have it done in the UK.

Partly out of fear and partly out of a profoundly arrogant disbelief that I could ever get cancer, I delayed the appointment. The pain continued for a while and in fact began to increase. This started me on a steady diet of ibuprofen.

Over the coming months, as the pain increased, along with my intake of ibuprofen, I continued to work, but it was getting harder and harder to function. I returned to London after working in Toronto before Christmas 2017 in more pain than ever. Felicity insisted I visit a doctor in London who specialized in cancer of the salivary gland. Within ten seconds of prying my mouth open with a gloved hand and looking down my throat, he said, 'You have a huge tumour at the base of your tongue. It is most likely cancerous, and this is what you are going to do. You are going to have a scan. This scan will most likely show that you have cancer and whether it has metastasized. Then they will perform surgery to remove it if they can. Then you will have radiation and chemotherapy and most likely you will have to eat through a feeding tube in your stomach for some months.' He had no bedside manner to say the least.

I almost fainted again.

In the hope of finding a cure for Kate, we had travelled around the world and met a number of doctors and scientists, some traditional, some alternative, who had dedicated themselves to finding a cure for what Siddhartha Mukherjee calls the emperor of all maladies, so I had come to learn about cancer from many different perspectives, and that knowledge had made me at once hopeful and very fearful. Because Kate's experience with the standard of care (chemotherapy, radiation, etc.) had been so horrible and ultimately futile, I was determined not to go through any of it.

The problem was that the tumour was so large, surgery was not possible as it would have required removing a large section of my tongue, ensuring that I would never be able to eat or speak normally again. Therefore, the only viable option was thirty-five days of high-dose targeted radiation and seven sessions of low-dose chemotherapy. Luckily, because the cancer had miraculously not metastasized, it had been proven that following this protocol meant the cure rate was close to 90 per cent with an extremely low rate of recurrence. Those were very hard figures to argue with. So, in the end I *did* go through with it, because I *had* to. I was, of course, terrified, and although she was such a proactive and positive force, I knew that Felicity was as well. And rightly so. She was pregnant, we were soon to move into a new home, and we had a two-year-old and three children in high school. Yet her innate fortitude, determination and intelligence to doggedly calculate the best way forward and find the most accomplished, avant-garde team of doctors whose treatments would assure a successful outcome eclipsed any fears she may have had. Her reassurance, love and patience were my greatest pillars of strength and still are to this day, in all things medical and otherwise. What a shame she doesn't feel the same about me.

At Mount Sinai Hospital in New York City, the head of the department, Dr Eric Genden, laid out the initial course of treatment, and Dr Richard Bakst took over my case from there. Upon meeting him it was evident that Dr Bakst had been given an extra dose of bedside manner upon his graduation from medical school. But no matter how kind and reassuring he and his team were, my greatest fear was that one of the most important and vital parts of my life would or could be severely compromised, perhaps permanently. That important and vital part being the ability to taste, eat and enjoy food.

How could they possibly expect me to willingly lose my sense of taste and smell and suffer the indignity of having to be fed through a tube in my stomach, the latter of which I was still determined to never be subjected to? They listened patiently as I expressed this fear over and over again in the form of countless questions, to which they always answered that, yes, indeed it would be hard going, and I would suffer the loss of my sense of taste and smell as well as most of my saliva, but it was more than likely I would make a full recovery in time. I didn't believe them. But I did. Except for when I didn't.

The Treatment

In order to undergo targeted radiation of the neck or head successfully, the patient's head must be completely still. Five days a week for seven weeks, a bespoke webbed mask would be placed over my face, my neck, and the upper part of my shoulders and then pinned to a board to completely immobilize my head during the sessions. A 'bite block' was then inserted through a hole in the mask and clenched between my teeth to keep my mouth and tongue also as still as possible. I was beginning to realize that, for better or worse, most major influences in my life come through this orifice.

And after three treatments I developed labyrinthitis, a condition from which I had occasionally suffered in the past. It is an extreme form of vertigo causing horrible nausea and the inability to do anything but lie down until it passes. Unfortunately it also caused me to completely lose my appetite just as the radiation was beginning very quickly to take its toll on my taste buds, my salivary glands, and the flora and soft tissue of my mouth. After a week of treatments, anything I was capable of putting into my mouth tasted like old wet cardboard. A few days later everything tasted like the same old wet cardboard but slathered with someone's excrement. A constellation of ulcers erupted in my mouth, as did viscous, wretched-tasting saliva. From this point on, day after day, all of the above just got worse and worse. The smell of any kind of food was repellent to me because it didn't smell like what it really smelled like. Only the worst components of food were what I smelled or tasted if I even dared put anything in my mouth at this point.

My inability to eat anything save a few sips of beef or chicken broth continued. I made attempts to find something in the fridge to eat, but even upon opening the door I was confronted with odours most foul. As I said, I could only smell the worst components of any given food, therefore each of those components in every carrot, carton of milk, orange and leftover roasted chicken sitting innocently in the fridge coalesced into a fetid wall of stink. I tried a few more times but soon ceased visiting the fridge and finally the kitchen itself entirely. If Felicity, who was very pregnant at this point but as strong as ever, entered the bedroom where I lay in a profound state of nausea, unable to even read, and if she had just eaten or had been cooking something, the odours that clung to her were so powerfully repellent to me that I would ask her to stand at a distance for fear of vomiting all over her. I was given protein drinks but could barely get them down. The morphine I was given to dull the pain and help me sleep caused such dreadful constipation that at one point I thought it might only be relieved by the use of a mini pipe bomb.

The irony was that while I was getting my chemo treatments once a week or getting intravenous fluids to hydrate me a few times a week in the hospital, I watched *cooking shows*. As they say or tweet, '*WTF?!*' This was an act of pure masochism, as even just the *thought* of food disgusted me. In hindsight I suppose it was a way to cling to what I loved or remember what I'd once had because I was so desperate to have it again. I was determined to make myself heal faster than any patient ever had. I would regain all of my sense of taste and saliva sooner rather than later, no matter what the doctors or statistics said, by watching *MasterChef*, Giada De Laurentiis, *Iron Chef*, *Diners, Drive-Ins and Dives*, and that gross, unnecessary show with the guy who eats as much of something as possible for no apparent reason and yet somehow still remains alive, because they were the fuel that was going to get me there.

Somewhere in the middle of treatments, actually on April 19, Felicity gave birth to Emilia. She was born by caesarean, which as we know is easiest on the baby and not so great for the mother for quite a while afterwards, although vaginal birth isn't exactly a thrilling experience either. (Let's face it, if men had to give birth, there would probably be only a total of about 47 people living on the face of the earth today as opposed to billions, and abortion clinics would be just another department in Walmart alongside auto parts, golf gear and firearms.) Luckily, I was strong enough to be present at the birth to see Felicity and our sweet issue afterwards, but I soon had to disappear into my bed again. I kept thinking I would regain my strength enough to hold Emilia and help Felicity, but by the fifth week I was so weak, was so nauseous, and had lost so much weight I practically begged to have a feeding tube implanted in my stomach. That tube was to remain in me for almost six months.

By the time my treatment had ended, I had lost thirty pounds (about two stone), had lost all of my facial and neck hair, and could barely walk up a flight of stairs. Upon our return to London, I had to stay in bed all day and feed myself through the tube, with either protein shakes or, eventually, food of my own making. I had missed cooking so much that I would struggle through the smell of the ingredients just to be able to stand at the stove and create something I knew I could eat. What it tasted like didn't matter, as it was going directly into my stomach by way of the tube, but it was important to me that if someone else were to eat it by mouth they would find it appetizing. I would purée beans and chicken stock with some pasta or even egg fried rice but had to thin it all quite a bit with water or more stock so it wouldn't clog up the tube. The tube was also the way I hydrated myself, as I could not even drink water by mouth because it burned like battery acid.

When confronted with my weakened condition, my older children, Nicolo, Isabel and Camilla, were very positive and encouraging. However, I knew how hard it was for them to see me so ill when, not even a decade before, their mother had suffered similarly. It was evident that my being diagnosed with cancer really frightened them, but Felicity and I reassured them that mine was a very different prognosis than Kate's. However, the trauma of losing a parent never fully disappears. Only the parent does. But I knew that no matter how much reassurance we offered, part of them feared that they would have to experience that trauma all over again.

Week after week, month after month, as Matteo's height and vocabulary grew, Emilia began to sleep through the night and learned to crawl, Nico and Isabel applied to universities and graduated high school, Camilla approached her junior year, we somehow moved into our new home, Felicity healed from her surgery, I slowly started to get better.

However, I will admit that it was a much longer and more

difficult recovery than I'd anticipated. I had suffered from depression during treatment, and even after treatment my depression continued for months. There were so many days when being confined to my bed, listening to my family go about their lives downstairs while I was unable to participate in any way, made me feel like a ghost in my own home. There were times when I believed I would never ever be able to cook or enjoy a meal again with the people I love.

Six months after my last treatment, I flew to New York City for a scan and stayed with our friends Ryan Reynolds and Blake Lively. (If you thought the name-dropping was over, I am sorry to break your rice bowl.) I wanted to go to the scan alone but Ryan insisted on coming with me. (He's the only pushy Canadian I know.) The team of doctors gathered around with the results of that morning's scan, which showed 'no evidence of disease' (now my favourite four words in any language). Needless to say I was greatly relieved. Ryan had tears in his eyes, as did the female doctors, but I know it was only because they were in such close proximity to him.

The doctors all agreed that I could finally remove the feeding tube from my torso, and I was thrilled. A balloon filled with water keeps the tube from slipping out of you and on to the floor, and to remove it one simply drains the balloon, grabs on to the tube, and gives a good yank, which I was told would feel like a punch in the gut, and that's that. I asked if we could do it then and there instead of waiting for the doctor who had inserted it. The mood was buoyant because of the good news and the presence of Mr Reynolds in the room, so Dr Bakst gave the go-ahead for the indecorous appendage to be removed. One of the female doctors, who like the rest of the staff, had been in a constant blush, including the men, since Deadpool himself had entered, said she would do the honours. Still in the amorous delirium of the starstruck, she grabbed the tube and was about to yank it from my wizened torso when I cried, 'Wait!'

'What?!' she asked, looking at me slightly annoyed because I had spoiled her big moment in front of you-know-who.

'Don't you want to deflate the balloon first?'

'The . . . ?'

'The balloon. Inside me. You have to . . . otherwise it won't fit through the –'

'Ohhhh, right, right. Yes. Of course. Sorry. I just . . . It's been a while since I've done it.'

Amid much laughter, she carried out the procedure properly and I was finally free of what had been my second mouth for too long.

Once that tube was removed I felt a profound sense of freedom. Now I had no other way of eating except through the orifice specifically designed for that purpose. Although I had already began to eat by mouth, my diet was limited to only soft, mild foods. This was frustrating, but I knew I had been incredibly lucky not to have lost the ability to swallow properly and move my tongue in a normal fashion, two side effects that are very common even without surgery, because the radiation can cause significant damage to the muscles necessary for both actions. Speech therapists are part of post-treatment programmes to teach recovering patients specific exercises to help them regain mobility in their tongue and jaw. Luckily four years of speech and vocal training made me hyperaware of what was happening and I was therefore able to do what was necessary to maintain normal movement along the way.

———

For over two years my mouth was incredibly sensitive. I couldn't drink anything carbonated and certainly could not eat anything spicy. I was able to drink and taste alcohol but mostly stuck to white wine with copious amounts of ice. Red wine also had to be iced, as the tannins made it feel like someone had taken a cloth sprinkled with dust and pepper and dragged it across my tongue. My beloved Martinis were a sad struggle. Steak was impossible because the lack of saliva makes one unable to break down meat enough to swallow it and thereby the whole bite turns into a bolus that is very easily choked on. (I had a few close calls attempting to eat something as benign as a chicken breast.) The same was true for most flesh and thick pieces of bread. Whatever I ate had to contain a certain amount of moisture in or around it, otherwise it took quite a while to get it down my throat or I just couldn't eat it at all.

It is fascinating how perfectly balanced the human body is. A little less saliva and the number of foods one can swallow drops precipitously. When I'd see my family members casually grab a piece of bread or a cracker, a piece of smoked salmon, or a few pieces of salami to slap into a baguette and wolf it down without a thought, I was so envious. For everything that entered my mouth, I'd have to calculate what I'd need to augment it with in order to swallow it without choking. Not unlike my father, I used to eat far too quickly. As a kid I would have finished my second dish of pasta when my sisters had barely finished their first. This bad habit disappeared out of necessity. I also could not casually chat to someone across the table while eating. For the most part, I had to finish the task at hand and *then* have a conversation.

Even when I was able to once again go to restaurants, have people over for a meal, or go to someone else's home for dinner, I was filled with anxiety because I didn't know what I'd be able to eat. I was afraid I would choke on something or eat something spicy by mistake and then not be able to eat for the rest of the night because my mouth would be in so much pain. If someone would ask me to taste something, whether it was a friend, a restaurant owner or a chef, I would try a bite just out of politeness and fake that I could either taste it or swallow it, or that I wasn't in agony. They could not understand or conceive of the fact that something so delicious might taste like shit to me or that even gentle spices might damage my mouth for the next twenty-four hours, or, for that matter, comprehend what it's like to eat anything having basically no saliva. Even at home I often found myself eating separately from my family because I was embarrassed about how hard it was for me to get through a simple bowl of pasta. All of this was frustrating and anathema to the way I had lived my life ever since childhood. How I socialized was primarily through eating and drinking. Although each week there was some progress, I could not help but feel that things would never return to the way they were, when life was edible.

As I said, for almost two years, with the exception of stocks and broths, I ate a primarily vegetarian diet. The following dish was a staple as it was easy to swallow and basically contained all the nutrients I needed to keep myself healthy. I can honestly say that after all this time I am still not sick of it because it's really delicious. This recipe, along with scrambled eggs, oatmeal and various soups, basically kept me going and helped rebuild my strength.

Pasta Fagioli (My Way)

– SERVES 4 –

Extra virgin olive oil
1 medium onion, sliced
2 garlic cloves, halved
½ bunch cavolo nero, roughly chopped
Three 400g cans of cannellini beans
750ml chicken stock (page 263) or vegetable stock
500g to 750g marinara sauce
500g small pasta, like ditali or gnocchetti sardi
Salt
Freshly ground black pepper
Parmigiano-Reggiano or Pecorino, for serving (optional)

- Pour a glug of the oil into a medium pot and sauté the onion and garlic over medium-low heat until soft. At the same time, boil the cavolo nero in a small pot of salted water.

- Add the beans, stock and marinara to the pan with the onion and garlic and stir together. Cook over low heat.

- When the cavolo nero is soft, strain it, add it to the bean mixture, and stir. Continue to cook on a low simmer with the lid askew for about 15 minutes.

- In the meantime, boil the pasta in salted water according to the directions on the package. When it's done, strain it, reserving about a cupful of the water, and place it in a large bowl. Add about 2 cups of the bean mixture to the pasta along with some of the pasta water and a drizzle of oil, and mix.

- Salt to taste and divide among four bowls. Add more bean mixture to each bowl along with a drizzle of oil. Sprinkle with pepper and Parmigiano or Pecorino, if using.

Variation: Loosely scramble 2 large eggs in a pan with olive oil. Then add one portion of the finished recipe above, including the pasta, and toss together. Finish with grated Parmigiano or Pecorino and a drizzle of olive oil.

There have been two rather strange beneficial effects from the radiation treatments, neither of which I anticipated. One is an increased metabolism. I already had a very fast metabolism, yet now mine could keep pace with that of my eighteen-year-old self. The other is that any food allergies I had, such as intolerance to dairy, sugar, and at times gluten, have basically disappeared. I have been told that because I didn't really eat for so long my system 'reset', as it were. It's like when people are told by dieticians to cut out certain foods to see if they might be the cause of some gastrointestinal issue, then slowly reintroduce those foods some time in the future and the stomach will sometimes be able to accept them. That has happened in spades to me. I can eat basically everything now, my digestion has never been better, and I have finally put on about fifteen pounds.

———

I have chosen to write about this painfully ironic experience because my illness and the brutal side effects of the treatment caused me to realize that food was not just a huge part of my life; it basically *was* my life. Food at once grounded me and took me to other places. It comforted me and challenged me. It was part of the fabric that made up my creative self and my domestic self. It allowed me to express my love for the people I love and make connections with new people I might come to love. When I was travelling, it kept me in touch with my family wherever I was in the world, whether on holiday or cooking for myself and a few colleagues while filming on location. During such meals I would explain that the recipes I'd prepared had been passed down through many generations. These humble dishes had travelled from Calabria to the US to London and now, to give one example, on location with me to a small bungalow in England's Lake District, where they nourished a whole new set of people who had just entered my life. Watching my guests enjoy the meal I'd made filled me with great familial pride. In those moments it was clear to me that some day, when my parents are no longer alive, I will always be able to put their teachings and all the love they gave me into a bowl and present it to someone who sadly will never have had the good fortune of knowing them. But by eating that food, they will *come to know them*, if even just a little. Until I began to fathom my deep emotional connections with food, I had always thought that the ceremonial eating of the communion wafer, a symbol for the body of Christ, was a strange, almost barbaric, pagan ritual. However, now it may well be the *only* aspect of Catholicism that makes any sense to me at all. If you love someone, you *just want them inside of you*. (I know what you're thinking, but let it go.) How many parents hug and kiss their kids and say, 'I love you so much I just want to eat you up!' Love can and does enter through the mouth.

I must admit that years ago I never thought that my passion and interest in food would come close to eclipsing how I felt about my chosen profession. Acting, directing, cinema and the theatre had always defined me. But after my diagnosis I discovered that eating, drinking, the kitchen and the table now play those roles. Food not only feeds me, it enriches me. All of me. Mind, body and soul. It is nothing more than everything.

Cook.

Smell.

Taste.

Eat.

Drink.

Share.

Repeat as necessary.

For better or for worse, those actions are now the definition of the person who is writing this. Were I not able to perform them, I would cease to exist.

In *Letters to a Young Poet*, Rainer Maria Rilke tells a soldier who aspires to be a poet and has sought Rilke's advice that (and I paraphrase) only if he feels like he would die were he unable to write should he be a poet. That made perfect sense to me forty years ago when I first read it, and it makes even more sense to me today.

———

As I write this, I can once again cook and enjoy meals with my family and friends, and although I cannot yet get through an *entire* T-bone steak, there is quite a bit I can eat.

Such as . . .

. . . sole meunière and *tortellini con panna*, risotto, pancakes, salami (slowly), *pasta alla carbonara*, shrimp fried rice, dim sum, a thin piece of toasted homemade bread with butter and jam, fresh-squeezed orange juice, tomato juice, young Pecorino cheese, honey, paella, Tuscan fish stew, asparagus, roasted peppers, Italian tuna fish packed in oil, fresh tomato salad with cucumbers and basil, gazpacho, scrambled eggs with smoked salmon, feta and cucumbers wrapped in a warm tortilla, chili con carne (extremely mild!), udon or soba noodles in broth, sheep's or cow's milk ricotta, tuna melts, razor clams, mussels, oysters, clams on the half shell, goat's cheese, langoustine, pasta Bolognese, Swiss chard, Felicity's roast potatoes (slowly and with lots of gravy), blueberries, pears, pizza, *zucchine*, eggplant parmigiana, anchovies (not too salty), pâté, olives, baked Camembert, minestrone, *pasta con piselli*, lasagna (not too cheesy), fresh peas, green beans, sautéd mushrooms, blueberry pie, baked beans, baked sea bass, lobster (mostly the claws, with a lot of melted butter), tarte Tatin, bouillabaisse, rabbit stew, beef stew, banana splits, cheese toasties, potato and leek soup, *pasta all'amatriciana* (not spicy), orecchiette with sausage and *broccoli di rapa* (slowly), chicken soup with matzo balls, caviar and blinis (if someone else has bought the caviar), a fried egg on a very thin toasted bagel, *pasta con pesto*, mashed potatoes, baked salmon, butternut squash soup, any kind of ravioli, *cappelletti in brodo*, mortadella and prosciutto (slowly), gelato, espresso, and so on and so on and so on . . .

But the most important thing is, I can finally *taste* it all.

All of it.

All of that food glorious food.

London, 2021

*I*am in the kitchen with my six-year-old son, Matteo. We are seated
on the floor doing a puzzle. Matteo is getting annoyed.

ME: Why are you so cranky?

MATTEO: I'm not cranky.

ME: Well, you are.

MATTEO: I'm not.

ME: Are you hungry?

A beat.

ME: Are you?

MATTEO: What?

ME: Hungry. Are you hungry?

MATTEO: I don't know. What do we have?

ME: What we usually have.

A pause.

ME: What would you like?

No response.

ME: Matteo, what would you like to eat?

MATTEO: Ummm . . .

ME: Would you like a sandwich?

MATTEO: Maybe.

ME: A salami sandwich?

MATTEO: Ummm . . .

A pause.

ME: Tell me.

MATTEO: I don't know.

ME: But you *are* hungry?

MATTEO: Yes.

ME: So, then, what would you like?

MATTEO: Ummm . . . I'm not sure.

A pause. I rise creakily from the floor.

ME: I'll make you a salami sandwich.

MATTEO: Can I have a jam sandwich?

ME: Of course. Would you *like* a jam sandwich?

MATTEO: Uh-huh.

ME: Pardon?

MATTEO: Yes, please.

ME: Come and sit at the counter.

Matteo moves lethargically and sits on a stool at the kitchen counter. I remove the jam from the fridge and bread from the bag. Matteo stares into the void. I open up the jar of jam, take a knife from a drawer, and am about to spread jam on a piece of bread.

MATTEO: Salami.

ME: Sorry?

MATTEO: Salami. I'll have salami. Salami sandwich.

I sigh.

ME: You'd like a *salami* sandwich?

MATTEO: Yes.

ME: You're *sure*?

MATTEO: Yes.

ME : All right. How do you ask?

MATTEO: May I have a salami sandwich, please.

ME: Of course.

I put away the jam and take the salami out of the fridge.

ME: What would you like on it?

MATTEO: Ummm . . . cucumber.

I look at him, my eyebrows raised.

MATTEO: Please.

I get a cucumber and a peeler and start to peel it.

MATTEO: Oh! Don't peel it!

I sigh, stop peeling, rinse off the cucumber, and begin to slice it. I make the sandwich with the salami and cucumber.

MATTEO: Can you cut off the cru –

ME: I am, I am.

I cut the crust off the sandwich and am about to cut it in half when Matteo shouts.

MATTEO: *NO!*

ME: What?!

MATTEO: (*meekly*) Can you cut it in triangles?

I sigh.

ME: Jesus, you scared me.

MATTEO: Sorry.

ME: Just two?

MATTEO: Two what?

ME: Two triangles.

MATTEO: Ummmm. Yeah. Yes. Two. Please.

I cut the sandwich into two triangles, plate it, and pass it to Matteo.

ME: There you go.

MATTEO: Thank you.

ME: You're welcome.

A silence. I watch my son eat greedily.

ME: Wow, you *were* hungry.

Matteo nods, cheeks swollen with sandwich. I smile. After a moment he speaks with a mouth full of food.

MATTEO: What are we having for dinner tonight?

ME: Pasta with tomato and peas.

MATTEO: Awwwww, nooooo!!! Do we have to!!?

I roll my eyes.

ME: Well, why don't you go next door and see what the neighbours are having?

Matteo sighs dramatically. I smile.

To be continued . . .

for generations to come all around the world . . .

Some Thanks.

Today, as I type this, I am almost completely healed. (I ate venison the other night, a little more slowly than I once did, but I ate it and I, well . . . I loved it.) Thanks to Dr Bakst and his team, including Bethann Scarborough, the head of palliative care at Mount Sinai; my friends; my family; and especially my wife, Felicity Blunt. After two and a half years, many scans, many workouts, and lots of beans, I have a clean bill of health. Fortunately, after three years, the likelihood of this type of cancer's returning is very low, and the chances of its ever rearing its ugly head again drop precipitously with each following year. I would also like to thank my dear friend Dr Niven Narain at BERG for his help in seeing me through it all.

During my recovery, I was so lucky to have our nanny, Martina Domanicka, and my assistant, Lottie Birmingham, with me, Felicity and Matteo in New York, as well as Andrea Galik, who looked after Nicolo, Isabel and Camilla in London. All three of those women went above and beyond to support us through what I hope will be the most difficult time in our lives. Without them and my loving in-laws Joanna, Oliver, Susie and Sebastian, Felicity could never have coped with a newborn and a bedridden husband as she herself was recovering from her caesarean. And even though Felicity was supposed to be on maternity leave, she still spent a lot of time working from home because she felt she was shirking her responsibilities to her clients. She was and still is utterly indefatigable. I hope my 'show-biz' agents and manager are reading this and learning. But I jest. I would also like to thank those agents and my manager, Tony, for being so understanding and encouraging.

How can I ever thank my parents for being so supportive from afar and when they visited after Emilia was born? I know seeing me so frail cannot have been easy for them. And thank you to my sister Gina, who came to visit me during treatment to cheer me up, and my sister Christine, who, from her home in LA, was always so positive and encouraging.

Thanks also to: My loving friend Alison Benson for housing me when I first arrived in New York for my initial tests, and my cousin Joe and his wife, Robin, for doing the same. My sister-in-law and brother-in-law, Emily and John, selflessly let us stay in their gorgeous home in Westchester during my treatment, ironically right near where I was raised and from where we had only moved four years before. This was an act beyond kindness for which they should be beatified. (I have been told that I can't personally beatify anyone, so I have made a few overseas calls. Seems it might be a bit harder now because of Brexit, but I am working on it.)

Ryan Reynolds and Blake Lively, who gave us their stupidly tasteful New York apartment for two weeks during the time Felicity gave birth so that we would be closer to the hospital. And I don't even know how to thank Ryan for being with me on the day of my first scan. I was, and still am, so happy he was there. Our dear friends Oliver Platt and his wife, Camilla, housed Martina and Lottie during that same two-week period. Without their generosity I don't know what we would have done.

So many friends came to visit me in the hospital or on weekends to try to lift my spirits, which was not an easy task, although I know it made the doctors and nurses very happy to have a parade of well-known beloved actors traipsing up and down the ward on occasion.

When I returned to London, a person who looked like Colin Firth would check in on me almost daily or take me to the hospital for check-ups and sit with me during hydration sessions. His support was invaluable.

When I was able to exercise again, our friend and Pilates teacher Monique Eastwood and our trainer Daryll Martin patiently helped me regain muscle and restore me to the level of fitness I had previously reached and then some!

How can one ever repay such kindnesses?

I guess I'll find out.

Oddly, some of them have been coming by lately around dinnertime.

For them, it's only about the food.

Gluttons.

Acknowledgements

First, my parents, Joan and Stan, for their love, encouragement and inspiration at the stove, at the table, and beyond.

My publishers, Jen Bergstrom and Helen Garnons-Williams, for believing I could actually write a book.

My editors Juliet Annan and Alison Callahan, for their unwavering care and patient guidance through my first literary effort.

Deborah Schneider, for her friendship and support.

Those chefs and friends who have inspired me, taught me, and allowed me to write about them and include their recipes here: Gianni Scappin, Pino and Celestino Posteraro, Adam Perry Lang, Massimo Bottura, and whoever that Italian bartender was who taught me how to make the perfect Martini all those years ago.

My assistant, Lottie Birmingham, for being the best friend and assistant ever in the world ever.

ACKNOWLEDGEMENTS

I especially would like to thank my wife and book agent (I never thought I would write that sentence), Felicity Joanna Francis Blunt, for her wisdom, patience, kindness, love and support, and her effortless ability to impart them to the likes of me.

POMODORINI